H

Succeed as

Single Par

How to Succeed as a Single Parent

Diane Louise Jordan

and Janice Fixter

Illustrated by John Byrne

Hodder & Stoughton
LONDON SYDNEY AUCKLAND

649.10243

British Library Cataloguing in Publication Data
A record for this book is available from the British Library

ISBN 0 340 86119 3

Typeset in Garamond by Avon DataSet Ltd, Bidford-on-Avon, Warwickshire

Printed and bound in Great Britain by
Clays Ltd, St Ives plc

The paper and board used in this paperback are natural recyclable products
made from wood grown in sustainable forests. The manufacturing processes
conform to the environmental regulations of the country of origin.

Hodder & Stoughton
A Division of Hodder Headine Ltd
338 Euston Road
London NW1 3BH
www.madaboutbooks.com

' "This is my Son, whom I love; with him I am well pleased" '
(Matthew 3:17)

Justine, you're precious and loved, and with you I am extremely pleased! Thank you for being an excellent daughter.

Contents

Acknowledgments

Thanks to Cav, Mike and Sam for their friendship; Ashana for the proofreading(!); Nathan and Natasha for living out commitment; Rae for your unrelenting loyalty and love in the bad times; and Mum and Dad for modelling unconditional love.

Huge thanks to my lovely co-writer, Janice – a woman of great tenacity, courage and integrity. It's been a pleasure working with you.

Greatest thanks to Sue, who it's impossible to thank adequately for her input, both into this book and into my life. I cannot believe I've been blessed with such an amazing friend. Ruth 1:16 is for you Sue!

Introduction

That Was the Week That Was

It was as a result of great loss that I became a parent.
Paradoxically this was also a time of great joy. Let me explain.

In April 1989 my sister, Jay, was fatally struck down by a
mystery flu virus just before her thirty-first birthday. It was
Good Friday, but on that particular Friday it didn't feel too
good. Jay had been a single parent. Naturally amid the mourning
and funeral plans, questions were raised about two-year-old
Justine's future, as her father was also no longer around. It was
at this time that I became acutely aware of just how loved this
little girl was – everybody in the family wanted to parent her! As
it was becoming increasingly difficult to reach a unanimous
decision about who should look after her, we decided that the
best course of action was to let Justine decide for herself. To my
amazement and delight, Justine chose her Auntie Diane!

Looking back, I now realise that this may have seemed a
rather strange way to deal with the situation, but Justine's
decision wasn't as odd as it might sound. First, I had been
sharing her childcare with my sister in the last months of her life
because Jay had returned to college, which meant Justine and I
had become used to spending a lot of time in each other's
company. Second, amid having to come to terms with Jay's
death, our family felt that it was important to provide stability
for Justine as soon as possible.

I'll never forget that week. I had begun it as an auntie and
ended it as a parent. But this was just the first of many huge

adjustments that Justine and I would have to make as we embarked on our lives together.

According to recent surveys, there are an estimated 1.7 million one-parent families in Britain – nearly a quarter of all families. Ninety per cent of single parents are women, but single parents of both genders care for a total of around three million children. I acknowledge that becoming a single parent in the way I did was, if not unique, at least slightly unusual. I also believe, however, that if we took a random cross-section of all the family situations up and down the UK where only one parent is resident, we would be amazed at the sheer variety of circumstances that have led to 'single-parent' households. For example, many will have become single parents through family break-up or bereavement. There are single parents who have never had a resident partner. You may be an adoptive parent like me, a teenage parent, or someone who became a mum or dad later in life – the list of variations goes on and on.

Family sizes also vary enormously. You may have one child or several. Whatever your situation, it's very possible that, initially, like me, you didn't set out to walk down the path of parenthood on your own. Even now as you sit and read these pages, you may still be wondering how you got to be here.

It is at this point, and with this in mind, that I feel I must dedicate at least one of these opening paragraphs to a confession. Nothing sordid, you understand; just the admission of the enormous responsibility I feel as I embark upon writing this book. I know that I simply cannot do justice to every family circumstance. Despite my best efforts, generalisation – filtered through my own experience and prejudices – will inevitably creep in. Some situations I describe may adequately relate to your own experience of parenthood; others may differ considerably and simply wind you up. I hope you will be able to draw something from the former and forgive me for the latter.

And, before moving on, two further caveats. First, I have

decided to use only the female gender when writing about a child – it saves all the grammatical gymnastics involved with phrases like 'tell him/her you love him/her' and, in any case, my experience makes it more natural for me to write about a child as female (I hope male readers will understand!). Second, my choice predominantly to use the phrase 'single parent'. OK, so I know it will grate with some of you – you may prefer 'lone parent', 'resident parent' or some other term (I'm sure there are more) – but if there is a phrase that adequately describes our situation and which is more widely understood than 'single parent', I have yet to come across it.

Going it alone

I was in the middle of a theatre tour at the time my sister died, and I left as a single woman to attend my sister's funeral. When I returned I was a single parent. The implications and responsibilities of parenthood didn't even occur to me; I just knew that Justine needed to be loved. So when friends repeatedly told me how heroic I was by taking on a child (especially at such short notice), I really couldn't understand what they meant. Of course now, thirteen years on, with the experience of motherhood, I do. With hindsight I'd say that I wasn't heroic but just unbelievably naive! I definitely made the right decision, but more through luck than judgment.

Justine was two when she became my sole responsibility. It would be wrong of me to give you the impression that everything fell into place from day one. It didn't. Justine needed time to grieve and adjust to the fact that her real mummy wasn't going to walk in through the door at any moment. I, too, was anxious about becoming 'replacement mum' – it felt disloyal to my sister. So what would Justine call me? And how would I describe my new relationship with her? All these things took time to work out. But despite coming together through tremendous loss, we faced the challenges together and I can honestly say that, as a result, the transition proved far smoother than I could have ever hoped for.

Other factors also played their part. For a start, the sudden impact of having a young person in my life and having to continue as a working mum left very few hours in the day for anything else. Justine was also thrown into a totally new way of life – one that was full of activity.

I was part of a Royal National Theatre tour of *The Pied Piper*, with performances in a different town every week. It wasn't unusual to have up to three shows a day. The company very generously organised a nanny for Justine at each town we visited. This proved to be a totally superfluous arrangement as Justine would often spend the morning and matinee performances glued to the 'prompt corner', completely transfixed by the activities on stage. During the evening performances she would happily sleep in my dressing-room. Perhaps this was not the ideal way to raise a child but, at the time, I felt that I had little choice but to make do. And as it turned out, for the remaining two months of the tour, this arrangement suited us perfectly.

I'm convinced that this period had a profound effect on Justine and brought about her love of the stage but, most importantly, it forced us to get on with life.

Support

Another reason for not feeling the plague of loneliness at this time was due, in no small measure, to the tremendous support we got from friends and family. In theory I was a single parent, but the reality was often quite different. While on tour I had members of the company baying for an opportunity to baby-sit Justine – even though all I ever wanted to do was spend *every* free minute with her. I had to fight them off! And my family and close friends all rallied round, often turning up unexpectedly to spend time with Justine and me on tour. This unrelenting support was a lifeline to me, especially in the early days, and continued even after the tour finished and we were on our own for the first time in our one-bedroom flat, surviving on unemployment benefit.

Justine and I also kept ourselves busy. Money was almost non-existent at this time, so between auditions we filled our days with hobbies – painting, going to the park, visiting friends and attending the numerous 'free' events that were on offer. We have a lot of good memories from this time. I know few children who don't get immense pleasure through drawing and painting, and Justine was no exception. I remember on one occasion we eagerly counted the days until the next benefit cheque. On its arrival we dashed to the local art shop to purchase a huge, purple, glitter crayon (to add to our collection) and spent that afternoon and well into the early hours of the next day creating a masterpiece on a large roll of lining paper. Our activities were punctuated with bowls of microwaved popcorn and catnaps. We had enormous fun (on a shoestring), and that weekend is still cited by Justine as one of her most memorable childhood highlights.

Two's company . . .

I tend to be a naturally optimistic person and, though I sometimes worried about lack of work, I made a decision. I resolved that while out of work I would spend every moment enjoying life with Justine.

Day bus passes and packed lunches were instrumental for great days out, sightseeing, kite-flying, and popping into free museums and art galleries. In truth, it didn't really matter what we were doing – what we both cherished was the doing it all *together*.

People often comment on how unprepared I must have been – i.e. not having nine days let alone nine months to prepare for parenthood. (Of course the advantages of doing it my way – no stretch marks, morning sickness and outsized clothing – were totally overlooked!) But, even if planned, nothing can really prepare any of us for the shock of parenting. And the sudden realisation that you're parenting on your own can be overwhelming.

It took a while for me to fully realise the responsibility, because (despite it arising out of a time of mourning) my being on tour with so many friends around created an extended honeymoon period. In fact I remember craving for time to be alone with Justine.

A lack of money and time to pursue adult interests are, I know, often major causes of concern for single parents. Funnily enough, our struggles didn't occur until I began working again. Then the struggle to balance time, energy and guilt hit me like a tidal wave. It was overwhelming and, like many single parents, I lost my self-confidence for a while. I lost confidence in the decisions I was making, began to ask myself whether I was a fit person to raise my child and also doubted whether the 'work-family balance thing' was really achievable. My self-confidence gradually returned, thanks to a network of people who continually reassured me and, as time went on, I settled into my new role as Mum. My daughter was two and a half when I adopted her but once life had settled down my feelings were similar, I suspect, to those of many new parents when they hold their baby for the first time. The responsibility seemed awesome and I felt quite inadequate.

Blue Peter

The day I landed the *Blue Peter* job was one of my happiest but it also marked the beginning of a very difficult time of being a parent. On the outside all looked well – my daughter had the best designer outfits and her mother had a glamorous, child-focused job that – allegedly – took up only half an hour of her time on Mondays and Thursdays! The reality was that although we had huge support from my mother and, of course, no money worries, most of my time was taken up with work.

On the rare family days out that we managed to grab, my high profile made it difficult for us to go anywhere without being mobbed by children. After a while we even felt robbed of the time we spent together. And of course, the demands of work resulted in Justine and me spending less and less time together. Gradually the complexities of parenthood began to haunt me. We began to hanker after the days of little money and endless time – how simple life seemed then. The truth is, of course, that very few of us can live for sustained periods of time with very little money. I wonder how long we could have really lasted living on the breadline. And how demented would I have become, constricted to a lifetime of picnics and bedtime stories?

The ideal family?

Few, if any, enjoy the luxury of feeling like the perfect parent – it's a feeling I find particularly difficult to even imagine – there are so many opinions about how to get it right and where we're all going wrong. The choice is endless . . . should we work, stay at home, get extra help, go it alone, be strict disciplinarians, allow our children to be free spirits, pay for professional help or draw on the support of family and friends, or just send our children away (boarding school/care, etc.) until they're eighteen and just meet up for skiing holidays and Christmas parties?

And what is the ideal family anyway? Families come in all shapes and sizes – adopted, fostered, extended, reduced . . . the list is endless. And the feelings that go with parenthood are also endless. Some people seem to take instantly to becoming a parent, while others take a little longer to warm up. Some of us may be enjoying every moment spent with our children; some of us may be completely exhausted by all the demands. But whatever the shape of your family and however you are feeling, our children need their parents – an adult who loves and cares *specifically for them.*

I love you . . . this much

Recently, I was watching a television programme that featured an experiment that revealed how children bond at a very early age with their primary carer (usually the mother), and how they withdraw and struggle to develop trusting relationships if that bond is broken. While watching it I was reminded of a well-known Beatles' song that claims 'All you need is love'. I remember thinking that it's relatively easy to put such a sentiment into a song, but putting it into practice is much more of a challenge.

Love is not just a feeling; it's an action – best expressed towards something or someone. So, perhaps the most fundamental way parents can show their children how much they are loved is to be with them as much of the time as possible – and to show our children that we *want* to be with them, that we're not just there out of a sense of duty. Our children need to know that we're interested in them and that we enjoy their company. We may find this difficult to believe, especially when our teenagers may only grunt at us, but they need to know that we are interested in their lives. They want us to spend time with them and be a part of their lives. They want us to understand them. They want to feel loved. When I started working I was soon made painfully aware that all the expensive gifts I showered on Justine were of little value to her – she just wanted me, her mum.

Just *being there* can be the greatest gift we shower on our children. The Rt Rev. James Jones, Bishop of Liverpool, says, 'The antidote to poor self-esteem is to know you are loved.' As parents, we can show that love by creating a stable, secure home environment for us to share with our children – a haven of security where they can turn to for love and reassurance, even during the sleeping hours of the night.

I know mine may not have been the most orthodox way of becoming a single parent – but whose is? Whatever your situation, this book tries to explore some of the common issues we face – and I hope it will offer a timely reminder that, even as single parents, we need not be alone in facing the joys and challenges of parenthood.

1
Help! I'm the Grown-Up!
Responsibility

When my sister was alive and we shared childcare I didn't fret if Justine refused a well-balanced meal – I knew she'd be returning to her mum who'd take care of that. It wasn't a problem. However, when I became Mum and Justine, aged two, declined – for six weeks, day in day out – to have anything but bananas and Ribena I was distraught. During one particularly stressful evening I remember thinking – here I am with one of the most sought-after jobs on TV, with viewers the length and breadth of the country envying my supposed 'showbiz' lifestyle, and the reality was that I was home-alone, reduced to a blubbering wreck by a child barely out of nappies.

Beside myself, I took Justine to the doctor, who reassured me that her behaviour was completely normal. Although I found his advice hard to take, within days, and with no explanation (!) she returned to a normal eating pattern . . . the little angel!

It has often been said that parenting is 'the most important job on the planet' but 'job' falls short of an adequate description for the most awesome, all-consuming responsibility any one of us will ever face. It's good to remember that we're all in the same boat – even the childcare experts can be flummoxed by their own child's behaviour! All parents make mistakes – it's a fact of life. Even the parents who look as if they have everything together will get things wrong. So, great parenting isn't about getting everything perfect – it's about trying to sort out the mistakes. It's like baking a cake without a recipe. You have an idea about what you hope to achieve and you start off with what you think are the right ingredients. Along the way, however, you realise you may have added too much sugar or not enough flour and you have to make adjustments. And then you realise that the cake might not turn out the way you expected so you have to add some more of this and that – and hope for the best!

Three sides to every story

There seem to be three main issues to caring, which are highlighted by many single mums and dads. They are:

1. The burden of sole responsibility – being alone and wondering if you're getting it right.
2. Feeling that your own inadequacies are affecting what you do but also feeling powerless to do anything about it.
3. Knowing that somebody's life is dependent on you – and you alone.

Realising that every parent experiences similar challenges can be a great comfort – we're not on our own. Recognising your feelings is a step towards keeping the burden in perspective. Fear of failure as a parent is a very common concern. And it's common to all kinds of parents – not just single parents. I have made *many* mistakes, and although I wouldn't choose to relive any of them I have certainly learned from those experiences, and today Justine and I are generally very happy. We have a great relationship. Recently Justine accidentally sent me a text message intended for one of her friends. In it she described me as a 'heavy' mum – 'heavy' (she assures me) being current teenage-speak for 'brilliant'! Well, I have a pretty brilliant daughter too. It hasn't always been this good though – Justine and I have had to face some fairly painful times. Yet as we've discovered, no matter how bad things have been it is never too late to learn from the mistakes and get back on track – even if you think all's completely lost. Often in life good things happen even in the bleakest of moments!

Tip for success
Recognising the responsibilities you face is a step towards keeping the burden in perspective.

Decisions, decisions

However you look at it, as a single parent the pressure is all on you to make the best choices. I've often pondered on how bizarre it is that for such a task there is very little preparation or on-the-job training. Thankfully, however, there are no on-going inspections to 'see how well you are doing' either! There is often no one on hand who can help you make a decision and we all know the old adage, 'a burden shared is a burden halved' so it's easy to feel especially weighed down by some of the choices you have to make.

Ruth was a single parent in a long-term relationship that finally broke down. All the time she was in that relationship, however, she didn't feel like a single parent because there was always someone around to talk and offload to. Decisions regarding her son had been made either by Ruth on her own or by her partner – never together – depending on how she was feeling. Once the relationship broke up, Ruth realised that she had opted out of some of her responsibilities as a parent by handing over choices to someone who, ultimately, wasn't that interested. Back on her own Ruth decided to be more consistent with her decision-making – regardless of any potential partner.

Parenting is not a nine-to-five job – you will be faced with tricky decisions at unexpected times of the day and night. For example, at what point do you call the doctor in the middle of the night when your child is ill? Your child is asking to go to a friend's house, a friend who you feel is a bad influence – what do you say? The choice, as they say, is yours – and yours alone. You may be fortunate to have a good friend or relative who you can ring at any time of the day or night but, on the other hand, you may just have to take a deep breath and decide what to do yourself. Whatever decisions we face, I've found it helpful to bear in mind the following:

- Be positive. Indecision cripples. Spending minutes, hours or even days swinging from one choice to the next takes an enormous amount of energy – energy that could be better spent elsewhere.
- Gather all the information you need and work from what you know rather than what you don't know.
- Don't spend a disproportionate amount of time making run-of-the-mill choices. If the outcome doesn't really matter, resist the temptation to waste lots of energy on it.
- Try not to let your imagination get carried away with what happens if you make the wrong choice.
- Once you've made your decision, move on. Don't waste time and energy worrying about whether you've done the right thing. You cannot change the past. However, if it's not working out, take time to look at other possible options. Remember that the majority of decisions we make are not one-way valves – there is often an opportunity to change your mind.
- When you are faced with big decisions it's helpful to talk to a friend – use them as a sounding board. Sometimes just talking it out can lead you to your own conclusions.
- If you really don't have anyone you can talk to then find a few moments of quiet, sit down with a pen and paper and write a list of pros and cons. Writing things down is enormously helpful – it serves to empty your head of the clutter so that you can actually see what you are facing.

You may find that the pros outweigh the cons, or vice versa. It may be a close run thing. Either way, you will be closer to making a choice.

- Don't be afraid of trusting your instincts. Have confidence in the fact that you're making the best choice from the information you have.
- As your child grows up remember to include her in the decision-making process.
- Never be afraid to admit you got it wrong. 'Sorry' is a word we could all use a bit more. Explain to your child that you blew it and say sorry. Tell her that you love her and want the best for her, then start again.

The 'lurve' thing

Loving our children is arguably our greatest responsibility as a parent. Thinking of love as a responsibility might be a strange idea. 'Of course I love my child' I hear you cry – but what does

HOW COME THEY CALL IT 'SINGLE PARENTING' WHEN THE WHOLE POINT IS YOU'VE GOT TO THINK OF SOMEONE OTHER THAN YOURSELF?

this really mean in practice? Loving someone is much more than indulging ourselves in soft, warm feelings – although there is a place for these too. Our love should be unconditional, no strings attached, seeking to serve our children in a way that helps them to grow to their full potential.

Unconditional love means loving our children when they do something wrong. You might not like the fact that your daughter has just smashed a window; you might be very unhappy with her, but don't let her think you've stopped loving her. As a single parent you might not have the luxury of another adult on hand who can console your child while you fume. An angry parent can appear to a child to be an unloving one – even if that's a million miles from the truth. It's helpful if you can be aware of how a child might view your reactions – 'Mummy doesn't love me because I broke the window' – and that's a scary idea when you're the only parent a child has. Talking helps. Tell your child that you are cross because of what she's done. Tell her you need time to cool off – give yourself ten minutes' breathing space before you decide what to do next. Once you've decided how you're going to handle the situation, do it calmly. Try to keep the lines of communication open at all times and go the extra mile after the event to show your child you still love her.

Unconditional love means loving your child when she's made a mistake; it means loving her just as she is and it means loving her when she doesn't live up to your expectations. It's really important that we love our children just as they are. We can have high hopes for them but that shouldn't affect, or even appear to affect, our love for them. Children can be very sensitive to what they perceive as expressions of love. A younger child might feel left out or not so loved when her older brother comes home with brilliant exam results and becomes the centre of attention. You may not feel any more love for one of your children in particular, but a child may think you do. As single parents, we may have to put more effort into showing that we love our children equally. When there are two parents, a child who feels left out can seek comfort with the other parent. When there is just one parent the child may have no one else to turn to. We need to develop antennae that tune into our children and pick up when they're feeling neglected and the way to do this is to spend time with them. In particular, those of us who have arrived at single-parenthood through bereavement or family break-up will be familiar with the added insecurity that children have had to cope with. Bear in mind that:

- A child who's feeling insecure may withdraw. Don't be tempted to let her get on with it but instead make time to find out what's wrong.
- A child who's feeling insecure may start attention-seeking. Any attention is better than none and can lead to bad behaviour. So if your child suddenly starts behaving badly, try to get to the root of the problem rather than dealing with the symptoms.
- Any change in your child's behaviour needs some investigation from you.
- If one of your children is in the spotlight and the others aren't, find a few moments to spend with each child on their own and tell them you love them.
- A hug and a kind word are often all it takes to make a child feel loved.

Tip for success
Unconditional love gives your child security.

In families there are always swings and roundabouts, and if you have more than one child you will know that there are times when one will receive more attention than the other – whether it be through sickness, or bad or virtuous behaviour. Overall, these times tend to even out, but be aware of them – make a special effort to show each child you love them especially if one is taking up more of your attention.

Loving our children ought to be really easy – but it isn't always. I once heard the lyrics to a song that said, 'Love is not a feeling, it's an act of your will.' If we're honest most of us have had to exercise that 'will' when we've been hard pushed to even *like* our offspring!

It's no sacrifice

Our children deserve our love for no other reason than simply because *they are* our children. They shouldn't need to 'be' or 'do' anything at all to gain our unconditional love. It's a tall order, isn't it? If I'm honest, I sometimes find unconditional love a bit daunting. It means giving up things – time, energy, activities you want to do – in order to spend time with our children. It's often harder if you're a single parent as you don't have a built-in baby-sitter in the form of a partner, so you will have to make choices about how often you go out. It won't be easy just to pop out – you will have to plan carefully, and planning takes time. We all need to make careful choices about how we spend our time.

Unconditional love isn't just about how often you go out – it's about listening to your six-year-old explain the finer points of a computer game when all you want is peace and quiet. You won't be able to tell your child to ask the other parent when it comes to homework time – that joy is all yours – unless you can get willing grandparents, aunts, uncles and your best friend involved (though not all at the same time!). Try to give your child as much undivided attention as you can. Spending a few minutes listening intently to your child is worth its weight in gold and you may well find that your child stops pestering you if you go out of your way to give her the attention she's looking for.

Tip for success
Make the most of the time you have with your child as she won't be tugging at your sleeve forever.

Care for the carers

There are times when those of us who care single-handedly for our children can feel very isolated. On a practical level there may be no one close at hand with whom we can share even the most simple, mundane decisions. We no longer live in tight-knit communities with family nearby, and we may not even know our neighbours. The entire responsibility is down to us. Sometimes it's exhausting. From the moment we get up to the moment until we go to bed it can feel there is so much to be done. Sometimes it's just like being on a hamster wheel – you feel as if you're the only one who can spin it and it'll all stop if you don't. There's no one to keep an eye on the crawling baby while you go to the loo! And as for actually completing tasks, that's pure fantasy! There's always washing to be done and meals to prepare and a thousand and one other jobs that you should have done last week.

There are no easy ways to lessen the sense of anxiety about caring alone. But as with all aspects of single parenting, try to build up strong relationships with those whose opinion you trust and who are willing to get involved with the nitty-gritty details of your life. Most importantly, trust your own instincts. Often there are no right or wrong answers when caring for your child; it's more a matter of working out what's best for both you and your child. You'll be surprised to find that so many of the small decisions you worry about now fade into insignificance as your child grows up.

Dave, a single dad, says this:

Before I was in this situation I was fairly intolerant of single parents. I just thought they were working the system and making the most of it really, a chance just to sit back and do nothing. There's still a lot of publicity about girls who get pregnant so they don't have to go to work, but once you're in the situation yourself it's a total eye-opener. I now think that those who bring up two or three on their own deserve a peerage!

Tip for success
Often there are no right or wrong choices,
just what's best for you and your child.

Be kind to yourself

Look for ways to take a break from the routine of life and give yourself a bit of space to breathe. If you're worn out – stop for five minutes and put your feet up. Don't feel guilty about the pile of shirts that need ironing – they'll wait. And who says they must be ironed anyway? Allow yourself a break whenever it's humanly possible. Five minutes can make a huge difference to your state of mind. It will help to ease the pressure. An ideal time with young children is when they are having a snooze or are happily occupied with some crayons. As your children grow older, share the fact that you need a break with them. You may only get five minutes, but it'll be worth it and you'll be amazed at how keen they might be to care for you.

Part of our responsibility is to accept that we cannot do everything all the time on our own. Try to avoid struggling on alone. Graciously accept any offer of help; if someone asks what they can do to help you, tell them! Don't be coy and struggle on alone. Hand out tea towels to anyone who offers. And don't be afraid to ask for help first. Pride and parenting are a bit like the proverbial 'blue and green' – *they should never be seen* together! I constantly ask friends and family for help and they're not avoiding me yet! If you're willing to take the plunge and ask, you may discover that your friends really do want to be involved in your life.

If asking for help really isn't your style, then try teaming up with other parents so you can help each other. See if there are any baby-sitting circles nearby. You may find that it's easy for you to do some baby-sitting in return for the odd evening off. Whatever you do, try to share your childcare with other people – no man is an island and none of us were designed to go it entirely alone.

A single parent I know called Monica has some good friends who are so attached to her son, Sean, that every year they pay for him to join their family on their foreign summer holidays. Sean gets a great holiday and Monica gets a break.

The other area to avoid is the one labelled 'Comparing Ourselves with Other Parents'. There are always going to be people who look as if they're doing a better job than we are – Sammy's dad is never late for anything and Joe's mum never has a hair out of place while you and I can't even remember where the comb's gone. Appearances can often be deceptive! Every family is unique and will have its own joys and disasters – it's not a competition. And if we compare ourselves with other people we will only ever feel two things – either a failure or smug – and neither are to be encouraged!

Tip for success
Never refuse offers of help!

The long and winding road

Our legal responsibility for our children ceases at eighteen but, as many an eighty-year-old will tell you, there's still plenty to worry about with fifty-something wayward children!

As a parent I'm responsible for the care and actions of my child until she is responsible for herself and, in time, for others too. Allowing our children to take responsibility doesn't happen overnight – it's a process or a journey where, bit by bit, we give them more choice about their actions. It is not something you can, or would want to do, all in one go. It has to happen slowly, over a period of years.

While we are on this journey, our aim is to equip our children to cope and be fulfilled at every stage of their lives. We can do this in a number of ways:

- Love and care for them
- Provide for and protect them
- Prepare and encourage them.

We obviously need to meet the basic provision of sustenance – things like food, shelter and warmth – but providing security for a child is enormously important and doesn't only come when it's packaged in a home with both parents resident. Rather it comes from *what* a child lives, not just with whom they live.

One of my favourite poems says this far more eloquently:

If a child lives with criticism, he learns to condemn.
If a child lives with hostility, he learns to fight.
If a child lives with ridicule, he learns to be shy.
If a child lives with shame, he learns to feel guilty.
If a child lives with tolerance, he learns to be patient.
If a child lives with encouragement, he learns confidence.
If a child lives with praise, he learns to appreciate.
If a child lives with fairness, he learns justice.

If a child lives with security, he learns faith.
If a child lives with approval, he learns to like himself.
If a child lives with acceptance and friendship, he learns
to find love in the world.

Let's face it, we would all love to live with someone who shows us tolerance, encouragement, praise, fairness, security, approval, acceptance and friendship – it would make a big difference to our lives. It is certainly demanding, but stick with it – true love is liberating, guaranteeing everybody an enormous amount in return. When your child has grown up and you have a relationship with her as an adult you'll be glad you invested so much in her when she was younger. And when our children are adults we can continue to show them how much we value them as part of our lives.

Look for the good

I wish I could learn to be more encouraging. Encouraging our children doesn't mean constantly dishing out spoonfuls of false flattery, but it does mean focusing on the good in a much more meaningful way. I once heard a very enlightened teacher say, 'Instead of trying to catch them "being naughty", I try to catch them "being good" and bring it to everyone's attention!'

I've witnessed first-hand the positive effect that teacher had on one little girl's life:

My friend's daughter Mimi was getting a reputation for being disruptive, which was beginning to become a self-fulfilling prophecy. The more she was reprimanded the naughtier she became. Then Mimi got a new teacher, Miss Sherwood, who actively looked out to praise her good deeds. Almost overnight Mimi was transformed. She is no longer disruptive and now loves school. Both her parents and the other teachers are bewildered but delighted with the new Mimi.

Mimi is a living example of how effective a few kind words can be. As parents we also have the ability to practise the power of positive encouragement – I challenge you to try it.

Tip for success
It's our responsibility to bring out the best in our children.

Sometimes all that's needed to change a situation is to change the way we look at it. Being angry and negative with Mimi produced an angry, negative child, but a little praise uncovered a willing, joyful heart. Whether we're parenting with a partner or on our own it is our responsibility to bring out the best in our children – to unlock the gem within.

Deliver us from evil

How many times have you heard a parent say, 'I wish I could take their place, I wish I could do it for them'? Exam time is definitely one of those times! When our children are young, the snares that await them are far easier to deal with; they are more obvious, and often of a practical nature, like ensuring there is a fireguard or a stair gate in place. The frustration intensifies as they grow older, however, as we realise that we are in fact powerless to protect them from hurt, both physically and emotionally. None of us want our children to experience pain and discomfort, yet wisdom tells us that we cannot wrap our children in cotton wool for ever. It is perhaps through such 'knocks' that they become stronger and empowered to take on the next hurdle. Our role as parents, then, is to prepare our children for the challenges of life and to let them know that, whatever they face, we will always be there for them.

If you love them, let them go . . .

It's a great joy to see your child grown into an adult and able to face the world. Letting go is never easy and perhaps for those of us who are single parents, particularly with only one child, an even greater degree of courage is required. However, few things will empower our children more than being prepared to step into their adult shoes, knowing that responsibility can be a gateway to true freedom.

2
Can Anybody Hear Me?
Communication

It started as an experiment. For one week Justine and I planned to go without television. How would we cope? What would happen? Would we just sit looking at each other in silence?

Guess what? We are now entering our third week and Justine doesn't want the television turned back on! She says that talking with each other is much better. And she's right! I've learned more about my daughter in the last few weeks than in the last few years. And I'm delighting in how fantastically lovely she is. Unlike the myth, which says that teenagers don't want to talk, I've discovered that my daughter's tongue is like a running tap – hurrah!

But that's only half the story. At age (nearly) sixteen Justine has spent most of her life doing what I should have done a lot more of – listening and observing. Justine knows me inside out. She knows my thoughts and opinions (of which I have a few!) on virtually every subject. In fact Justine could describe me fairly accurately.

On the other hand, because I've spent most of her life talking at her, instilling in her my values, thoughts and desires, I've allowed myself very little space to get to know my own daughter.

Until now! I've recently discovered the art of listening and we're now encountering a role reversal. Justine won't/can't stop talking (obviously compensating for the 'silent' years)! And I'm positively revelling in hearing all she has to say.

At long last I've finally heard what the experts have been saying for years – that communication is much more than talking to someone. In fact talking often hinders it.

'Communication' – every parent's secret weapon!

Communication is fundamental to successful parenting. Crack this code and many of the other challenges we parents face will greatly reduce.

I FOUND THE KEY TO SUCCESS AS A SINGLE PARENT WAS ACCESS TO INFORMATION!

HEY, THANKS FOR THAT INFORMATION!

The dictionary defines communication as a 'means of *transmitting* or "*receiving and giving*" information'. Essentially it's a *process* between two people, the essence of relationship. Sounds straightforward? As we all know, it rarely is. How many times have you got hold of the wrong end of the stick? How many times have you had conversations with people, knowing full well that they have no idea what you are talking about? It happens all the time. Communication isn't just a flow of words – there's non-verbal communication too. In fact most of our communication is non-verbal – facial expressions, hand gestures, shrugging shoulders, eye contact, or lack of it – we all know how much a gesture can communicate at an appropriate moment. I remember hearing a story about a little girl who, frustrated at her dad's lack of communication from behind his paper, shouted, 'No, Daddy! Don't you know you have to listen with your *eyes* as well?' And we've all had difficult conversations on the telephone when we're unable to read those non-verbal signals. Our body language gives us away; it communicates what we're really feeling and it's a really important part of the way we communicate with our children.

Tip for success
Communication is the key to a good relationship
with our children.

Body talk

When we talk to our children it's important that our body language tells our child we are ready to listen. If you have your back to your child or if you have one eye on a newspaper or a magazine your child will know that she doesn't have your full attention. Of course, we can't give our full attention to our children all the time but there are moments when it really matters. Your child needs to know that you are really listening to what she says – she will automatically read the signs that say you're not.

Peter's son comes to stay with him at weekends and during school holidays. He has found communication to be the key to their relationship.

My son, Oliver, lives with his mum most of the time but he spends weekends and most of the school holidays with me. It can be particularly difficult when I don't see Oliver because it probably takes a weekend to get good communication back – it can take until Sunday. It takes about a day and a half for us to settle back in, and actually that's been one of the key areas of problems for us.

I think communication is absolutely the key thing. The bottom line is spending time one on one. And eye contact is so important. You should really have eye contact. It's import-

ant to reflect back, to be a reflective listener. When I don't see Oliver for say, ten days, and a whole host of things have happened – he's changed. There's always a kind of remaking of the relationship in the early part of our getting together.

So how do we communicate successfully? It's virtually impossible to communicate successfully with somebody who isn't there so, in order to have a chance of effectively communicating with our children, it's critical that we start by spending time with them. It's far easier sharing thoughts and feelings with someone you really know and, out of the time you spend together, you'll be amazed at the new things you learn about one another. We'll be much better equipped to help our children grow if we get to know them and allow them to get to know us.

Tip for success
Spend time getting to know your child.

Do I know you?

With our busy lives, especially when we're juggling the responsibilities of work and home on our own, it's easy to slip into a routine whereby we discover that we're sharing our home with complete strangers. So don't allow your children to become estranged from you; spend time with them. If your child is as perceptive as my daughter Justine and most children are, she'll know quite a lot about you already (especially if she's had to suffer the one-way communication traffic that Justine has). But however naturally perceptive our children are it helps to be honest with them – tell them how we feel. Share the events of your day, both good and not so good, but always being mindful not to burden them.

- Make time to *listen* to what your child has to say – even if it's a blow-by-blow account of your eight-year-old's day at school.

- Talk with your child about what interests her – find out what makes her tick. What has she enjoyed about the day?
- Tell your child about your day and how you're feeling. You may be amazed by what she has to say to you.
- Do you really know your child? Do you know what her favourite colour is? What her favourite place is? Her favourite toy? The name of her best friend? Her favourite pop group? The list is endless. There are so many things we think we know about our children . . . and then they turn round and surprise us!
- Find out what your child thinks about *you!* A fun way to get to do that is to play a game. Take it in turns to describe each other as an animal, a vegetable, a type of transport, a material – and anything else you can think of. Be prepared not to take offence! I have a friend whose child described her as a racoon and a radish!

Out of the mouths of babes

> *Ruth was feeling really stressed out. She'd had a really hectic day at work and then come home to hit the after-school activities run. She had to be in three places simultaneously and hadn't been able to grab more than a cup of tea while she organised Cub uniforms and dance shoes. After half an hour of whizzing round in the car she ended up alone with her nine-year-old son, Luke. 'I'm feeling so stressed out,' she said to him, 'I just don't know how I'm going to get through the evening.' Luke looked at his mum who was near to tears and calmly replied, 'All you've go to do is think about one thing at a time. Don't worry about what comes next.' It was the best thing anyone had said to her all day!*

Spending time with our children doesn't always mean organising and planning some sort of excursion or activity. In these times, when it's usual for family members to isolate themselves from one another with televisions and computers in bedrooms, spending time can quite simply mean sharing the same room with the television off.

An American survey discovered that, in 1992, a typical child watched seven hours of television per day, spent an average of five minutes a day with his father and twenty minutes a day with his mother – and most of that was either eating or watching TV!

The television can be a handy occasional childminder – there are moments when we're desperate for five minutes' peace and a favourite programme is on. There are those, however, who believe that some children take their behaviour models from television – particularly those whose parents don't spend time talking to them. We've all heard the comments about violence on the television leading to violent behaviour in children. It's a contentious issue. I suggest that you don't let the television become a substitute parent. Control it rather than let it control you and your child. Be aware of how much and what your child is watching and be prepared to discuss some of the things that you see. Television can be a great way into some difficult issues but never be afraid to turn it off!

I've been meaning to tell you . . .

As a single parent there are issues and questions that you may find particularly difficult. How does a dad tell his daughter about periods? How does a mum talk to her son about the facts of life? How do you discuss boyfriends/girlfriends? Your approach will very much depend on the sort of people you and your child are and how easy you find it to talk about these things. Some parents will sail through this area with few problems; others find it more difficult. You may find it especially difficult if your own parents shied away from talking about sexual/personal matters. The following ideas may be useful:

- You will not have the same experiences as your child but that doesn't mean you can't talk about issues from your own perspective.
- Talk to a friend/relative who is the same sex as your child – maybe a parent with a child of a similar age – and find out what their approach would be.
- Try to be aware of what your child already knows.
- Playground talk means that children know more than you give them credit for – though they may not have all the facts straight.
- Be aware of what your child is being taught in school in PSHE (Personal, Social and Health Education). You may find your child is more receptive to talk through issues with you if she has been talking about them with her class.
- Try to pick a good time to chat – not when you're both stressed.
- Don't jump in with both feet. Take things slowly and see how open your child is to talk to you about the facts of life and relationships. Be prepared to give as much information as your child wants to hear, but bear in mind that she may not be ready for the full 'conception-to-birth' explanation at one sitting!
- Be honest. If you really can't face this sort of discussion tell your child that you find it difficult. One possible option is to ask a relative or a good friend who is the same sex as your child to have a chat. It might be an idea to discuss this option with your son or daughter instead of springing it on them.
- If your child clams up on you, don't take it as rejection or feel that you're inadequate – she may be as embarrassed as you.

It's also important to see these types of conversations as part and parcel of your relationship with your child rather than as

ONE OF THE FACTS OF LIFE IS THAT DAD GOES BRIGHT RED EVERY TIME HE TRIES TO TELL ME THE FACTS OF LIFE...

something out of the ordinary. Your conversations should grow and develop as your child does and at a pace with which she's comfortable – don't overload her with information! It's great to talk about personal matters when there are natural opportunities rather than having a 'let's sit down and have a chat' type of moment.

Tip for success
Look for natural opportunities to talk about difficult issues.

Silence can be golden

Communication isn't just about speaking – there are times when we communicate volumes by not saying anything. As the song from the film *Notting Hill* says, 'You say it best when you say nothing at all'. It's important not to underestimate the value of quiet times, especially in this world of wall-to-wall noise. We are bombarded with all sorts of sounds all the time. Where can we go to escape the ringing mobile phone? Or the buzzing from a CD player plugged into someone's ears on the bus? Whenever you can, make use of the rare, quiet occasions. Long car journeys are excellent opportunities for naturally induced periods of silence. It's surprising how silence can encourage your child to focus on the important things she forgot to tell/ask you. I've learned many profound things while driving down the M1 with the stereo off!

Silence is a very powerful way of communicating, and it can speak volumes to our children. It can be negative – 'I'm angry and I don't want to talk to you.' But it can be hugely positive – 'I'm here with you, ready to talk when you want to.' It can also be a companionable silence when there is no need to speak at all. It's often in sharing these silences that we learn masses about our children and they about us. If our relationship with our children is based on honesty it's likely that they'll find these times reassuring – so treasure them.

Tip for success

Make time to listen to what your child has to say.

Banana skins

There is, however, a banana skin waiting to trip us up and send us flat on our faces. It's important that we don't fill these quiet moments with nagging. Your child is a captive audience and you may have the odd, overwhelming urge to remind her that you haven't seen her bedroom floor for several months because of the bits of paper and unwashed clothing strewn across it. Or you may feel you have a golden opportunity to 'encourage' your child to work harder at school. There is a time and a place for both these conversations but a golden opportunity to simply enjoy each other's company and have a wide-ranging, two-way conversation is not to be missed. And what's more, if you nag your child whenever you have a few quiet moments together you'll soon be wondering why the quiet moments no longer happen.

Just a little respect

I'm naturally a champion nagger, so I try to kerb this tendency by considering Justine as I would a friend. I show my friends how much they mean to me by:

- Having fun with them
- Listening to their news
- Trusting them and confiding in them
- Looking out for them
- Considering things from their point of view
- Getting to know them better through their other friends
- Just relaxing with them.

In short I try to show them how respected and valued they are and that I want to be with them. Although I know that my primary responsibility with Justine is not to be her friend – first and foremost, I'm her mum – I know that it's crucial for me to communicate to Justine just how significant and appreciated she is.

You're the one that I want

We don't stand a chance of reaching our children unless they know that we *care* about them. A recent survey carried out by the National Family and Parenting Institute revealed that 'most people of all ages believe that making children feel loved and cared for is the best way to raise happy children'.

A great way of showing our children we care is by carving out special time for them. If you have more than one child, try and regularly spend time with each of them on their own – even if it's only a quiet bedtime chat. Make the most of any opportunity that presents itself – however unexpected. You may find your child hovering round you while you're busy cooking tea or doing paperwork. It's easy, when you've got so much to do, to brush your child aside and say you'll talk to her later – the reality is that 'later' often never comes. If you haven't really talked to your child for a while it's a good opportunity to stop what you're doing for a few minutes and show that you care for her.

MUM IT'S TIME WE HAD A TALK ABOUT WHY WE NEVER HAVE TIME TO TALK...

If you can, try to take time out away from home as a joint treat. Justine and I try to have a meal out together once a month. Sometimes it's really hard to timetable in, but it's always invaluable as we have an opportunity, away from the domestic routine, to indulge in getting to know each other again. But be warned! Avoid the temptation to use an evening out as an excuse to nag or complain. This tendency can pop up in the middle of all our well-meaning intentions! Bite your tongue if you have to. The only agenda should be a great night out. (Believe me, I've had to learn this the hard way!) And remember, to make this work well, only treat one child at a time if you can. The meal doesn't have to be expensive – I don't know any child who'd resist an invitation to one of the well-known cheap burger chains that we spend most of our time persuading them to avoid! It's not the quality of the surroundings but the quality of the *time* that is important.

However, if time and money are really tight (and you both hate eating out anyway) you can use any everyday family activity to stay close. Bike rides, making a meal together, running errands, walking to school, are all excellent opportunities for special one-on-one time.

Family times are also essential – occasions when everyone can get together in a relaxed way. In our home, mealtimes are mostly about being relaxed with each other. We sometimes have games evenings too, and these are also great times for relaxing together (unless of course I'm losing at yet another game of chess . . .). Some families are known to have more formal gatherings as well, when all family members have an opportunity to air opinions or/and grievances. This works well if each member of the family is allowed to have their say (including the parent) and is not interrupted or harangued. For some children, just knowing there's a special time for getting things off their chest helps reduce frustration, and teaches them how to listen, discern and be generally aware of the needs of others.

Tip for success
Show your child you care for her – not just with words but by the way you treat her.

To love you is to know you . . .

Will, a friend of mine, told me about the time that he threw a huge and flashy sixteenth-birthday bash for his eldest son, Tim. Will's parents had done the same for him and he remembers how much he loved the party and how it confirmed their love for him. So for his son it was to be a no-expense-spared affair; virtually everybody in the address book was invited. However, Will had overlooked one crucial detail – Tim hated being the centre of attention. Far from feeling overjoyed and much loved, Tim was mortified. His ideal birthday treat would have been a quiet night out with his dad and two closest friends.

One of the things we need to learn about our children is what they are thinking and feeling. A common tendency is to project our feelings and motives onto our children – I'm an expert in this area – but the trick is not to do it! We should never cease striving to understand our children. The only real way to do that is to spend time with them, listening to what they have to say. And remember our children change, we change too, so getting to know them is a long-term project. The child we thought we knew really well at five will certainly be a much more complex person by the time she's fifteen.

Selective hearing

So, what happens when the five-year-old who would talk a hind leg off the donkey becomes the fifteen-year-old? It's a common experience for a parent to sometimes feel as if they are speaking to a brick wall. At an undefined age, selective hearing begins and your little angel, who would once respond to your every smile, no longer hears your requests. The myth is that teenagers are a strange breed who find communication an alien experience. The truth is they're no different to anybody else. Push the right buttons (and I admit this can sometimes feel like searching for a needle in a haystack!) and you'll find that teenagers love to talk – they just have to have a really interested listener. If they hear only orders they may not be quite so eager to talk. After all, would you?

Sharon, a single mum with one son, summed up the situation like this:

I was pulled up short recently when my son Ben pointed out that all I ever do from the moment he wakes up until the moment his head hits the pillow is shout out orders: 'Get up or you'll be late for school'; 'You must have breakfast, you won't be able to concentrate all day'; 'You're not leaving the house like that'; 'You're not wearing that coat to school'; 'Where's your homework?'; 'Make sure you come straight home'; 'Who are you on the phone to now?'; 'Wash your hands before you eat your dinner'; 'Look at me when I'm talking to you'; 'Do your homework'; 'You've been on that computer long enough'; 'Turn off that TV, you'll not get enough sleep and you'll be tired in the morning'.

ONE OF THE PROBLEMS WITH 'SOLE RESPONSIBILITY' IS NOBODY MAKES THEMSELVES RESPONSIBLE FOR TEACHING YOU THE ROPES!

It's not just teenagers who sometimes have difficulty expressing themselves. The tantrums of a two-year-old may not be that far apart from a teenager's sulking. Whereas your two-year-old's tantrum may be the frustration of not being able to express herself adequately, the sulking of your teenager may be the manifestation of not being *allowed* to express herself. As parents we need to work out continually what our children are really trying to say – to search for what's happening underneath the surface. Sometimes this may mean patiently waiting and not rushing into any kind of action. Remember that children go through phases in their development and in their relationship with you. These phases frequently pass without you having to do anything about them. Try to avoid the temptation to feel that you're doing something wrong as a parent. Peter, a single dad who shares custody of his son, told me this:

> *Recently my son went into a massive 'reject Daddy' mode – I don't know where it came from, I don't know why it started and it ended as mysteriously as it begun. But what I had to do, however painful, was just say, 'Fine'. Eventually the phase ended. It's very easy, if you're being rejected, to overcompensate – buy things; be more attentive; do more, whatever it may be; be less disciplined for a while. But being prepared to simply sit back and keep the lines of communication open is the answer. Just keep saying 'It's OK, it'll be OK . . .'*

Tip for success

Give your child time and space to express herself.

It's never, *never* too late

The benefits of good communication are recognised far and wide. Even when you really believe there's no hope, try not to give up – we owe it to our children to always keep trying. Our love for them has to be unconditional. The Wessex Youth Offending Team was part of a national pilot scheme whereby 284 parents were summoned to court and given a parenting order on behalf of their children. The order required parents to have parenting lessons . . . and while some of them were initially angry, they soon realised that the scheme was there to help them to become better parents, not punish them.

The parenting lessons helped them to share their feelings and talk about the problems they'd been having. The parents learned to be less confrontational and to keep the lines of communication open – a vital key to improving any relationship. One mum said afterwards that it helped her enormously to realise that she was not alone in the problems she faced – and as a result of the parenting order her relationship with her fifteen-year-old son changed dramatically and for the better.

Real families are hard work and a successful one isn't a by-product of a hectic lifestyle – family life has to be worked at every day. Every day we must love and care for each other and show love in the daily tasks we do for each other. And above all we must communicate, whether it's with words or with a hug. However much else we have on our plate, we must aim to keep the lines of communication open at all times. Loving words don't cost us anything.

Tip for success
It's *never* too late to start communicating.

The language of love

'I love you' are probably the most powerful words we can say to our children. And these three words can never be said enough – although you may find it easier to tell a younger child rather than an older one that you love her. Get into the habit when your children are young and you'll find it's not such a big deal to continue as they hit their teens. And if your child is older and you haven't told her you love her, remember that it's never too late to start – we'll always be able to find a time and a place if we look hard enough.

3
What Do You Want?
Needs

I recently asked Justine to make a list of some of the things she'd most like to do. And to my amazement, far from being an outrageously impossible list, what she actually wanted and needed were, in the main, very possible and refreshingly simple. Her list covered the obvious, like increased pocket money and parties, but to my surprise it also included staying in and playing chess with me (very shrewd 'cause I usually lose!) and spending more time with our closest friends. We haven't yet attempted everything on the list but the incredible discovery I've made is that by attempting to meet Justine's needs, many of mine have been fulfilled too!

We all have needs – whoever we are – from the moment we are born. We all require certain basic things. Ask any parent of a newborn baby and they will be able to list the basic human needs we all have from day one – food, drink, comfort, love and warmth. As children grow it seems that this fairly simple list grows faster than they do. Before we know where we are it includes shoes, money for school trips and trendy haircuts. As parents, we have to keep on our toes in order to meet the seemingly endless needs of our children. But our success shouldn't only be measured by how much we meet our children's needs while totally disregarding our own, or vice versa for that matter. Rather, as in so many things, we need to find a balance.

What exactly do you want?

A good place to start working out how to get a balance in our lives is to go back to basics.

It is important to learn what our children's needs are, be they physical, emotional, mental or spiritual. As your child grows her needs may seem to be more complex but in fact they all stem from the same needs she had as a baby – she needs to be loved and cared for. How that need is expressed will vary from child to child and will change as she gets older. Some children need more attention than others, some need to be cuddled a great deal while others prefer more space. Some children will need a lot more help with their schoolwork. Different children in the same family will need your attention in different ways, so much so that, at times, you may feel as if you need to be several different people rolled into one.

Being aware of what makes your child tick will help you to know how to respond to her as an individual. Ask yourself:

- Is your child a touchy/feely child who wants lots of hugs?
- Does she seek approval and acceptance through verbal affirmation?
- Does she ask for help with things just to have you near?
- Does your child like space to be on her own?
- Does she ask you lots of questions just because she needs to talk to you?

There's no doubt that children do take an awful lot of effort. Listening to Justine, on the days she rushes in from school with the gory details about who's got off with who, wears me out! But she needs me to listen – even if I don't really care about who's with whom this week! By listening I'm showing my child that I care about *her* and what *she*'s interested in.

Justine, by her own admission, responds very positively to physical touch, acts of kindness and quality time. Our quality time doesn't always mean organised activity, but often opportunities just to be lazy together. Some of our most treasured times are days spent relaxing on my bed in our dressing-gowns, reading and eating. It is important for me to be aware of Justine's particular needs, so that even in a full and busy working day when I may feel stressed and perhaps not very tactile, I'm still able to show her how much she's loved. It's not unusual for Justine to be doing her homework next to me while I'm working, during which time I often consciously stop to give her a hug and a cup of hot chocolate!

All our children really need is our love and support expressed in a variety of different ways, according to their temperament. It's important that we are realistic in how we can meet these needs. If we understand what makes our children tick then we are less likely to waste time and energy doing things which they are really not that bothered about. When time and energy are at a premium for us it's especially important to get it right. Meeting the vast majority of children's needs isn't an enormous task. It's a series of moments strung together. My own experience has proved to me time and time again that happiness is found not in the big things, but in the small things in our daily lives. Quite often these small things are right under our noses – we just need to be trained to see them. (In my

experience, our children are desperately pointing them out to us, but we're too busy providing for them to notice their real needs). As Nick Page enthuses in his inspired book, just keep it simple! (See *Keep It Simple*, published by HarperCollins in 1999.) Check out the book if you want to learn more about how to get rid of the clutter in your life and find happiness in the small things.

. As parents it should be our aim to nurture our children and provide a stable, loving environment in which they can flourish. As the many phases of childhood change and develop, so do our children's needs – though stability and love are central to every stage.

Tip for success
Take time to find out what it is your child *really* needs.

I want ...

As your child grows you will be presented with a list of wants dressed up as needs. Picture the scene. A dad in a supermarket, pushing a trolley with his seven-year-old daughter in tow. The dad wants to get the shopping finished as quickly as possible because it's Friday evening, he's been at work all week and he's tired. He tries to hurry past the shelves stacked high with videos but it's too late. His daughter has spotted the latest video, the film she didn't see at the cinema but which most of her friends saw. When the dad says, 'No, you can't have it, we'll try and rent it', the daughter retaliates with 'But I *need* it'.

The words *I need* always trigger a response in a parent. How can they not? We want to provide for our children's needs – we don't want to let them down – and as single parents it's all up to us so we feel doubly responsible. If we don't provide, no one else will. It's easy to fall into the trap of feeling that we must get everything our child says she needs – however much it might cost us. After all, the responsibility is ours alone.

Melissa, a single mum with three children, expressed it like this:

> We live in a throwaway society – we throw away our cars, we throw away our clothes, we throw away our furniture. We throw it all away to fill up with more junk, and we do that with our families too. Material things are a burden – you know we need a television, we need a VCR, we need Nike trainers, we need, we need, we need. Now I've fallen into the same trap. Single parents can feel that their children don't have the same things as two-parent families. We need to realise that we don't need to give children those things – they actually need so little – and what they need most is to feel loved and have the room to grow. Throwing money at the children is not the answer. Stability is – even if you're struggling on benefits.

Both adults and children alike get bouts of the 'I wants' (I'm a little prone to this myself . . .). As single parents it's easy to feel particular pressure to give in to our children's demands and spend money on passing phases that we might not be able to afford.

There is no easy answer, but it's important to be clear about the difference between *wants* and *needs*. Your child may claim she needs a brand new pair of £80 trainers because that's what everyone else is wearing, but you'll have to weigh up how much she really needs them. Our children, on the whole, live in a very affluent society – much more so than ever before. They are swamped with advertisers telling them that they need certain products in order to look great, smell great or have a great life. It's difficult for us all not to be seduced by the growing pressure of consumerism – not to be enticed into believing that our children really do need those trainers in order to be accepted by their peers.

I'm fully aware of media/advertising manipulation and, as a

WE REALLY NEED TO HAVE A CHAT ABOUT THE DIFFERENCE BETWEEN WANTS AND NEEDS

principle, adamantly refuse to buy into it. In reality, though, it's a balancing act. For our children, fitting in with their peer group *is* an important part of their development and they may see that new pair of trainers as a key to acceptance. It's much harder to remain resolute when your child is in floods of tears simply because she wants her friends to like her. As parents, therefore, we need to balance our children's wants with purchases that we feel comfortable with and can really afford.

I'm an avid fan of *The Simpsons,* and I remember one episode in which Lisa pesters the President until she gets the response she wants. She eloquently sums up what many children know is so often true – if you cause enough fuss you'll get what you want in the end. Or as the President says to Lisa, 'You've taught kids a valuable lesson. If things don't go your way just keep complaining until they do.'

Unfortunately, teaching our children the difference between wants and needs is not something we can do overnight – it's part of a long process. The important thing is to make sure that we get into the habit of explaining the decisions we make, rather than just saying 'yes' or 'no'. Taking time to communicate to our children why we are responding in the way that we are, will help them in making their own decisions as they grow older.

And in the meantime, my only advice is to deal with requests on a case-by-case basis – after all, there will always be another 'must-have' around the corner.

Lucy spent years trying to teach her daughter Naomi to be aware of the difference between wanting something and needing it. When Naomi was fifteen she had an opportunity to go to Romania during her summer holiday to do some voluntary work with some street children. Naomi returned home with a whole new perspective. 'We don't need all this stuff to be happy,' she said to her mother, 'all the stuff we think we do. The kids in Romania just needed food, shelter and someone to love them – that's all they needed to be happy.'

Tip for success

Encourage your child to work out the difference between
I want and *I need*.

Spaced out

'I just need some space.' This has almost become an overused phrase by many of us in this manic, crazy world where we hardly come up for air. We seem to live such helter-skelter lives where we have to cram in more and more every year. The truth is that our children, whatever their age, quite frequently feel the same. They are rushed from childminder to school and home again and then out to after-school activities. Wherever they go they are surrounded by people, looking after them, teaching them. Children are no exception to the rule and need space just like the rest of us – although it's easy to forget when we're caught up with rushing round just to provide for them. It isn't just teenagers who need 'somewhere to be themselves'. Every child needs somewhere where they are allowed to express who they really are. Circumstances may limit the 'space' to the corner of a shared bedroom or an area of a communal room. It doesn't matter how much space your child has as long as she has somewhere to be on her own.

Space isn't just physical, though. Your child might need mental and emotional space away from her siblings but might want to share that space with you. When I was a child I would often be found playing with my 'cut-out' dolls alone in a corner of our very busy lounge – even at seven years old I sometimes needed to be 'alone' near my mum.

Tip for success
All children need some space to call their own.

Sometimes children will feign illness just because they want to have a day at home, hopefully with you. You know the signs. Your child wakes up with an undefined stomach-ache but isn't actually sick or showing signs of a temperature. You have half an hour to decide what to do and a day at work that you can't afford to miss. Invariably you end up sending your child to school and feeling guilty about it or taking the morning off work and feeling exasperated by your child who is bouncing round the house like Tigger. It's another tough call, but remember that, deep down, your child probably appreciates more than you realise the tension that you live with. Such instances, however, may serve as a wake-up call for you to concentrate – at least in the short term – on spending more time with your child.

Gary's partner died leaving him to bring up their daughter, Ashleigh. He's unable to get to all Ashleigh's school events, however much he would like to. He is very aware that this causes problems for Ashleigh and sometimes she says she's ill just so that she can spend more time with him:

I have a pretty good relationship with my daughter, Ashleigh, but what does affect her is that she doesn't have a mother picking her up from school. And things like school plays and sports days that your child wants you to go to. Ashleigh sees other children's parents and doesn't see hers and it can be very upsetting. I try to get to as many school things as I can, but you have a certain amount of holidays and a certain amount of time you can wangle, and there's a lot we'll both miss out on.

One of the hardest things I find is when your child tells you she's ill in the morning. You can't even ring up your childminder if your child is sick, so you really are stuck. I don't know if there are any statistics to this but I would imagine that children of single parents who are working have fewer days off school sick than other people's children because you just shove them off to school.

The other thing is when your child says she's ill and you don't believe her but psychologically she may just need to be around you and just have a day off, but you can't let her. Or you think that she may be really ill and so you take the morning off and then about ten minutes later she's completely fine.

If (or should I say *when*) you're suddenly aware that your child needs some extra attention you could try the following:

- Try not to think of your child as being awkward/naughty just to get your attention.
- If you can, clear all commitments and plans for the evening so that you can spend time with your child.
- If possible, do this for several evenings if that's what's needed.
- Plan something special for the weekend – it doesn't have to be extravagant.
- Talk to your child and try to find out if anything in particular is bothering her, but don't expect her to open up

straightaway – it may take time.
• Explain to your child how you feel about not having as much time together as you would like.

Buffers

Although you may be the only parent in your child's life you don't have to be the only adult. Your child will need other adults in her life to talk to. You needn't necessarily be the sole source of comfort and advice. Sometimes the intense relationship between a parent and a child means that the child needs to be able to offload elsewhere. Your child may need to confide in someone else – a trusted adult who your son or daughter can easily talk to. Grandparents are often really good in this role of buffer as they are one step removed from the everyday challenges (as are other family members such as aunts and uncles). There are many grandparents who are totally committed

to their grandchildren. If you don't have parents around to talk to your child, think about who else she could talk to. Other buffers can include close friends – surrogate uncles and aunts – or even a teacher at school. In fact a buffer can be anyone you trust and who you know loves your child and wants the best for her.

One of the great things about encouraging your child to talk to another adult is that they will offer her another perspective. It's easy to get bogged down in the parent/child relationship and for your child to think you're the only parent in the world who is making crazy decisions. If your child can chat to someone else it will broaden her horizons and hopefully help her to see why you make the choices you do – it may help to diffuse any difficulties that arise between the two of you.

Developing these sorts of relationships, as well as relieving you of some of the day-to-day stresses, can be really useful for your child too. There may well be things that your child would prefer to discuss with somebody else – at least initially. There are also occasions when a child needs to talk to another adult because she feels that talking to you about something specific will upset or worry you and wants reassurance that it won't be as bad as she fears.

It's easy to feel threatened if your child talks to someone other than you – we do tend to think we should be able to solve every problem single-handedly. The reality is that it's not healthy for us, or our children, if they can't talk to other adults. By giving your child the freedom to talk with someone you both trust, you'll be doing both of you a big favour.

Tip for success
Encourage your child to talk to other trustworthy adults.

Justine will, from time to time, choose to talk to my best friend, Sue, rather than me. Similarly Rachel, Sue's daughter, will sometime confide in me rather than her mum. Both girls know they can speak to either of us in confidence and, enticing as it is, Sue and I resist the temptation to pry. However, there have been occasions when the girls have told us something that we feel the other parent should know and on those occasions, we've encouraged and helped them to find a way of sharing the information with their own mum. There may be friends or relatives who can play a similar role by making themselves available for your child and you, and who are simply waiting to be asked. I know not everyone has the idyllic luxury of this arrangement, but my main point is that it's OK for your child to turn to other responsible adults.

What about me?

So what are the more obvious needs of a parent, especially one parenting on their own? Support, comfort, conversation? What you need most of all will depend on your circumstances. The one thing that all single parents seem to need, regardless of how they have arrived at their current situation, is more energy. A report recently said that a parent will lose 450 hours of sleep in the first year of a new baby's life and, believe me, as the parent of a socially active teenager, it doesn't stop there!

One of the best things you can do for yourself is to make sure that you get the basics right – eating properly, engaging in moderate exercise and getting as much rest as is humanly possible. You cannot run on empty for long. If you are forever chasing around it's easy to neglect your own fundamental needs in favour of your kids. Make sure that you eat enough to keep you going rather than constantly promising yourself you'll eat later. When you have no one to share the responsibility with, preparing food can become a chore, one that gets skipped over whenever possible. However difficult it seems, few would disagree that if you look after yourself properly, you'll be in better shape to meet the demands of parenting.

On the emotional front, you, as a parent, might feel the need to be looked after – to feel an arm around you at the end of the day, or have somebody you can actually talk to on your level. Talking on the phone just isn't quite the same as having somebody in the same room. You may have to be quite clinical and honest about what your needs really are – and realistic about which ones can be met.

What we want, what we really, really want . . .

We all are social beings, designed to be in relationship with one another. It's quite normal for us to want to be cared for – this is a fundamental human need. However, it's unlikely, and probably unhealthy, to have all our social needs met through just one person, and very unhealthy to look to our children to fulfil all our needs. It's essential that we take a realistic view of what we need, and from whom. If we centre our lives exclusively around our children, we may be in danger of making them feel responsible for our feelings. How many of us have heard stories about sons and daughters who still live at home well into adulthood simply because they feel too scared to leave their

parents on their own? We are failing our children if we put this sort of pressure on them.

All of us, not just single parents, struggle with loneliness from time to time. That said, the sense of isolation which stems from parenting on our own means that, perhaps, we are more prone. If I'm honest, there have been occasions when I have really missed having a partner but I've always tried to avoid using Justine to compensate for my loneliness. We mustn't make our children our best buddies because we are alone. Our children need us as parents, however well we may get on. They need friends of their own age – and so do we. So, particularly as a single parent, we need to nurture other adult relationships – it may take a lot of effort but it will be worth it in the long run. Try:

- going out of your way to make friends with people at work
- talking to other parents at the school gate rather than hurrying in and out
- arriving early to drop off/collect your child from preschool/nursery/after-school activities so that you can chat to other parents
- finding out if there are any local groups for single parents.

When you sit down and think about it, you may be surprised by just how many people you already know. True, some of the above might require a bit of co-ordination but arranging an occasional baby-sitter, even if it's planned well in advance, will provide you with the chance to go out and meet new people.

You may want to feel needed for yourself rather than for your function as a parent – so also try to spend time with people who value you for who *you* are. Members of your family, close friends and/or other single parents may fit the bill. It may be worth mentioning here that the grass isn't always greener on the other side. Remember that two-parent families aren't always better off than those with one – there are many families with both parents where emotional needs aren't being met at all. It's easy to believe that life for 'dual' parents is one joy after another – but it's not always true!

> ### Tip for success
> Spend time with people who value you.

Who wants to be a martyr?

It's healthy for our children to recognise our needs, and we certainly shouldn't feel guilty about letting them know that sometimes we make decisions just for ourselves. As Susan Jeffers says in her book *I'm Okay, You're a Brat* (Hodder & Stoughton, 1999) – I love that title! –

> *Where is it written that you must support the ambitions and needs of everyone in your family, but never ask for the same in return? And teaching them to respect the fact that their mother [father] also needs time and space is a valuable lesson.*

Being a parent is the best job in the world – it's also time-consuming, frustrating and demanding too! So don't get hung up about the fact that you have needs to fulfil as well; you may well deserve a break! If you want to write, or paint, or simply have other adult company, you should be able to do those things too – they just shouldn't always supersede your role as a parent. It's vital to be who you are – enjoy your personality! You're not being selfish if you create space in your life to pursue things that are just of interest to you. Your children are important and so are you.

> ### Tip for success
> Being realistic about our own needs means that we will avoid physical and emotional 'burn-out', which will help us to be more effective parents.

4
Pushing the Boundaries
Discipline

As a child, my sister and I enjoyed the enormous privilege of travelling to Jamaica to spend our summer holidays with our grandad. My grandad's style of living was a world apart from our council house in Hatfield. His love for us was unquestionable but his ideals of right and wrong were very defined and his boundaries crystal clear. I learned many valuable lessons from those long, hot, Jamaican summers, lessons and ideals that formed a strong moral foundation upon which I have been able to draw on, years later, as a single parent . . .

We are all role models – whether we're keen on that idea or not. Whatever our approach to parenting, the truth is that our children look at us for an example. We can instruct our children in all sorts of different ways, we can tell them what they ought and ought not to be doing, we can be a mine of information about manners – but at the end of the day it's our actions that speak louder than words. Our children look at the way we behave and the way we react and this is what they imitate.

As they grow older our children might be significantly influenced by their friends, but don't underestimate the impact that we still have upon them. They will still watch the way we act. If there is a gap between what we advise our children to do and what we actually do ourselves, our children will spot it! Words are empty without actions so, when it comes to boundaries and discipline, remember:

- If we want our children to learn self-discipline then it's important that we demonstrate how it works.
- It's back to the 'Here's one I made earlier' model – we have to actually *show* our children how to behave, step by step, not just issue them with a list of instructions.
- And if we don't behave in a way of which we are particularly proud, as responsible parents it's probably time to take a good look at our lives and the way we live.

Eating words

I wonder how many times before becoming a parent you, like me, found yourself saying, 'I'd never let a child of mine do that' and I wonder how many of us have been forced to eat our words. I know parents who were convinced their children would always look clean and tidy until they had them! The reality is often very different from the ideals we hold. We imagine life running smoothly and never imagine our children leaving the house wearing odd socks – but it happens! Our ideas about what we think is acceptable behaviour end up changing when we have our own children. Like so many issues surrounding parenting – and, perhaps, especially single parent-ing – discipline and boundaries present a whole host of difficult decisions as we often find our thoughts and feelings challenged by the world around us, not to mention by our children themselves. Few issues surrounding parenting are black and white, so we need to begin, as always, by looking at ourselves and being scrupulously honest about our own value systems – good and bad – and what's *really* important.

I want to praise you like I should . . .

When was the last time someone told you how wonderful you are? Or told you that you'd done a really great job? And how did that make you feel? For some reason we seem to be brilliant at pointing out each other's faults and weaknesses, and hopeless at congratulating each other on a good job well done – it seems to be something to do with human nature. And after all, most of us are painfully aware of where we fall short – we don't need to keep hearing about it! A few kind, but *honest,* words often work wonders.

When it comes to discipline we need to remember that:

- It isn't just about telling off; discipline is about providing a positive framework in which our children can thrive.
- Praise is the most powerful of the discipline tools. While there are times when you have to tell your child that she's done something wrong, there are also lots of times when you can tell your child that she's done something right!
- We need to give our children something to work towards – rewarding them for positive changes in their behaviour rather than constantly nagging them.
- When we do need to use punishment, it should be consistent and appropriate to the 'crime', and our reasons should be communicated clearly to our children.

Tip for success
Praise and reward are far more useful methods of discipline than condemnation or criticism.

Some people might call it bribery but my friend Clare swears by bartering with her children to get results. For example, she'll say to her eldest daughter, 'If you work really well at school I'll buy you a new outfit' and it works wonders! In fact she claims that it works much better than all the years of her saying, 'No, no, until you get it right you're not getting this . . .'

It's important to note that Clare rewards her daughter for working hard rather than achieving high grades. What we don't want to do is put our children under enormous pressure to achieve – if we do that then we're actually saying that they are worth more from us if they get an A grade. That sort of approach can end up spiralling downhill so that we end up with children who have to achieve in order to feel good about themselves.

As adults we often end up promising ourselves 'treats' when we get through a particularly difficult piece of work or difficult patch in our lives. Or we promise ourselves something as a celebration! The treats might be fairly simple things, but a bit of encouragement to work does not go amiss – regardless of what a child ends up achieving.

I recently read an article that said we criticise 90 per cent of the time and only praise 10 per cent of time. It's a depressing thought – just think what would happen if we could turn those statistics round so that we are positive and encouraging 90 per cent of the time!

Look on the bright side

We are often very quick to focus on weaknesses. One of my failings has been to concentrate on the things that have been going wrong rather than the things that have been going right. For example, when Justine comes in from school with a really good piece of artwork but has forgotten her gym kit it's the gym kit I've focused on first, not the amazing piece of art she's done. It's an easy trap to fall into! And once we've uttered the criticisms first our children won't be in a mood to receive any praise. So we need to stop and think before we speak. We need to praise children for the great things they've done before we nag them about smelly PE kits.

I'm also guilty of harbouring bad feelings – even about something as trivial as a forgotten gym kit. I have even been known to ruin an entire evening by sulking over something completely unimportant in the whole scale of things.

> **Tip for success**
> Don't hang on to your anger – remember you're the adult.

My grandad used to say that you discipline the child for what he's done and then you drop it the minute it's been dealt with. He lived by his word. He'd tell you off or give the appropriate punishment and then the subject was finished – as if it never happened. My grandad has been a great role model to me and his advice helped me see the power of forgiveness. His wise words have helped me to lay down the mantle of anger (forgiveness is addictive once you start – you don't want to spoil the joy of it by staying angry for too long). And that, along with being able to spend more time with Justine, has resulted in an amazing change in our relationship. I enjoy enthusiastically praising her over the good things that she does, and in turn she enthusiastically returns the praise. We've both gone the extra mile and it's definitely made a significant difference – *and* we both feel so much happier.

If I could start all over again I would pray for more patience and tolerance and I would definitely praise my daughter more.

Setting boundaries

Knowing exactly where to set boundaries in life is a daunting prospect. As adults, many of us aren't certain that we've got the boundaries right for ourselves so what steps can we take to ensure that we are successful in setting the boundaries for our children? In fact . . . why should we set them at all? Wouldn't it cause less grief in the long run if we simply adopted a more laissez-faire attitude?

Well, have you ever imagined life without laws? How would society operate or agree about anything? How safe would our roads be if there were no speed restrictions? How safe would our homes be if we had no laws governing property? The fact is, we all need boundaries, and families are no different:

- We need to know when we have crossed the line and said or done something we shouldn't.
- We need to be able to respect each member of the family as an individual and give them the room they need to grow and develop.
- Children need to know that we love them and that we have rules to protect them.
- Boundaries enable family members to live happily together, forming frameworks that accommodate all family peculiarities, likes and dislikes.

Do you really care?

Children, in particular, crave structure and consistency. Recently I saw a television programme about life on a very deprived housing estate in the north of England. I will never forget the response of the nine-year-old boy who, when asked what he most wanted in the world, answered, 'I would like my mum to tell me what time to be in, in the evening, like the other children.' Boundaries show that we care, and that little boy obviously thought he didn't matter – because his mum didn't seem to care what time he came home.

Every child, however, is different and will respond differently to the boundaries we place around them. We need to encourage our children, when they're old enough, to work out the boundaries with us. Even with the best will in the world we can sometimes give our children the impression that their choices are irrelevant; either we think that they are not mature enough or we simply don't care about their opinions.

It might be useful to sit down and even now (it's never too late) ask yourself: *What are my values?* List out your values – the principles that you think are important for life – so that you will have a clearer idea of where you want the boundaries. If you're not sure about what is really important in your life you will find it very hard to convey a clear value system to your child. We flounder and our children become confused when we keep changing the ground rules. Before becoming a Christian, I was always changing my mind about what I thought was right and wrong. My beliefs now give me a much clearer set of values, and, although I still struggle, they really help when making difficult decisions.

Keep on moving

It's also important to routinely reassess our boundaries. Family life never stays still – all family members grow and develop (adults included!). It goes without saying that some of the structures we put in place to keep a two-year-old safe are not necessary for a ten-year-old. The literal ones, such as stair gates and safety catches, are obvious and easy to see but the boundaries we set in terms of behaviour can go unnoticed and unchanged for much longer than they should. Unfortunately being a parent is not like being a workman who can spend a few days banging in fence posts, fix a long-lasting fence, wipe the sweat from his face and know that he's done a good job that will last a lifetime! As parents we have to keep on moving those boundaries and giving our children and ourselves a bit more space to grow.

The boundaries you set when your child is three should stretch naturally as your child grows. When Justine was five I couldn't imagine ever letting her walk to school on her own – but now there are lots of things she does without me. As parents we need to allow our children to grow in a safe environment – one which expands as they approach adulthood. If we fail to expand our child's boundaries, we risk smothering them. By recognising that boundaries must change we seek to understand their needs and by doing so give them vital tools to use in the world they all too soon will face without our constant intervention. We pass on to them the ingredients for their own success.

You may need to go back to your child and say, 'Look, I've thought about this and, although I've been adamant, I think you could be right.' Never, ever be afraid to admit to your mistakes! Change is not a sign of weakness; it's a natural and vital part of life. Don't be afraid to discuss boundaries with your child as she grows up:

- Make the decisions together – where you can.
- Ask her what time she thinks she should be in bed on a school night, before offering your own point of view.
- Ask her how late she thinks she should be allowed to stay out on a Friday night – it's a starting place for a discussion!
- If you can work out an agreement between you, your child is more likely to abide by the rules you've laid down.

Tip for success
Expand your child's boundaries as she grows.

Traps

There are two traps in the area of boundaries that we can fall into. There is the trap of being so busy that we never make time to sit down and think through the boundaries we are setting for our children – and then there is the other extreme whereby we say, 'Here are my boundaries. I have hammered them in place and they shall not be moved!'

We should try to avoid both, if we possibly can. If you're unsure about the discipline decisions you make – find a friend or relative to talk to. Don't be afraid of voicing your concerns to someone – every parent worries whether or not they've got it right and you'll find talking things through can help enormously. The majority of parents have the same worries and concerns over the decisions they make – none of us have the answers, we just try to do the best we can. As a single parent, find someone you can use as a sounding board – other parents with children the same age are great as they're in the same boat as you and are probably facing the same issues.

Give and take

One of the things I wanted to do most when I was a child was stay up late or stay up all night – because that's what grown-ups did and I wasn't allowed – and it was so exciting! Even the girls in Enid Blyton books had midnight feasts. How many children do you know who are always pushing for that extra half-hour before bedtime?

A child's messy bedroom is another classic example of boundaries being pushed against. With Justine I have had to make choices between allowing her freedom and keeping the rats out of her bedroom. Do I give her complete freedom, try to gently persuade, or do I really lay down the law? As a naturally messy person myself, I have to be careful not to be a complete hypocrite!

The reality is that there's often give and take on both sides. I allow Justine some creative (!) freedom in her room, but when she occasionally becomes overwhelmed by the clutter, I help to clear and reorganise. There are also times when she helps me reorganise my space. If any of us have a mountain to climb and someone genuinely comes and climbs that mountain with us it's much easier and far more pleasant.

Battles

Boundaries, however reasonably applied, will inevitably be kicked against, tested and, at times, fought over mercilessly. Without doubt some boundaries are definitely worth defending more than others – so pick your battles! There are some battles worth fighting with your child and some – let's face it – that are just not worth the fall-out. You might not like the idea of your child having her belly-button pierced but, in the grand scheme of things, is it worth damaging your relationship over something (literally) so small? Some battles end up draining everybody's energy and leave the whole family feeling grumpy and dis-satisfied. Other battles have to happen as our children kick against the limits we set. Of course, some will kick more than others, but all will struggle for their independence.

Sometimes it has to be us who take a big mouthful of humble pie. We need to be prepared to back down if we're the ones stubbornly digging our heels in unnecessarily. Remember that children learn by example, so our children will benefit from seeing us gracefully backing down.

Tip for success
Choose your battles. There are some battles which have to be fought, but others are just not worth it.

Peer pressure

Probably the hardest thing for any parent is to swim against the tide of peer pressure. It's also really hard for a child to stand out from the crowd. Never underestimate peer pressure – it's an enormous thing. You'll hear from your child that 'It's not fair, everybody else is doing it'. But that is no justification for you to break rules which you have already laid out. (The reality is that most children are uttering the very same words to their parents!) If you're not happy about a certain sleepover or a party that your child wants to go to, have the courage of your convictions. If you don't want your child sitting up watching horror films – don't let her. Take time to talk to your child and explain your reasons. She may still think you're barking mad but hopefully she will respect your point of view.

ET phone home

Take mobile phones! An issue I've struggled with recently. To me, mobiles encourage the culture of secrecy – hundreds of call and text messages are being sent all the time in our home. Morning, noon and night there's the happy sound of beeping that says, 'Message received' – it's the culture that older children and teenagers operate in. (Apparently young people spend 20 per cent of their money on mobile phones – but that's another story!) For a considerable period I felt it completely unnecessary for Justine to have a phone. However, the time came when keeping contact with her while she was out became essential for her safety and my peace of mind, and so the day arrived when that boundary had to shift. It was important that Justine realised I hadn't simply given in to her continual pleas for a telephone but had reassessed the situation and had acknow-ledged that both her and my needs had changed. I have also had to accept that the bombardment of text messages and phone calls are part of today's youth culture . . . how such things are funded is a separate issue. I can see how the way I interacted with friends in my youth has been partially replaced by the use of telephone waves! My friend Steve has had a similar experience:

> *A mobile phone encourages my fourteen-year-old son to have something that's apart from our relationship and it's raised a crucial point about letting go. Our children are going to face a whole world out there that we are going to know nothing about – so the issue is really about trust. Do I trust my child in the world he is creating around him? In allowing him to have a mobile phone I've extended one of his bound-aries – do I trust him within those boundaries? We need to trust our children unless or until they break that trust. It's no good setting the boundaries and then breathing down our children's necks to make sure they're sticking to the rules. It can be a hard lesson for us parents to learn.*

If we trust our children within the boundaries we've set then we'll be doing them a big favour – we'll be giving them an opportunity to learn for themselves. If we are forever making the decisions for them and hemming them in with rules they will not learn how to trust themselves – and they will not develop confidence. After all, if someone was peering over our shoulder checking our every move, our self-confidence would end up in shreds. It's hard for any parent to take a big breath and a step back and give their child a bit more freedom. But once we've done that we have to let them get on with it – we have to trust them.

Tip for success
Trusting children instils confidence in them.

Self-discipline

Our long-term aim should be to encourage our children to develop their own boundaries – to help them develop *self-discipline*. After all, you won't always be around to show the red card so the quicker your child learns to regulate her behaviour herself, the easier life will be for everyone. You may have an urge to control every aspect of your child's life, but try to resist it. Start off by encouraging your child, as soon as she's able, to make simple decisions herself – which clothes does she want to wear? You can build up slowly to the life-changing ones such as 'Is he the one for me?', over a very long period of time!

Encouraging self-discipline over homework is an issue that all parents face. A single parent has the problem compounded by the fact that we're often the only ones, in the home at least, doing all the nagging about getting work finished and in on time. Angela, a mum with two children, had particular problems with one of her daughters over the homework issue.

My daughter, Yasmin, spent much of the last year struggling with ill health but has still managed to maintain good school grades and fairly high spirits. However, the other night I discovered Yasmin had left a thousand-word essay, due to be in the next day, to the last minute. She had been given two weeks to complete it in and so was potentially in hot water. On discovering the spot she was in, the temptation was to become really angry but I had to say to myself: 'Think about how hard Yasmin works and how unwell she often feels. Look at what she achieves against the odds. Instead of coming down hard on her, perhaps I should tell her how well she is doing, address the issue and help her to be more self-disciplined next time.'

In the morning when Yasmin got up (after I'd helped her to finish the essay), I said, 'Look, I'm a bit disappointed because you had this homework set two weeks ago and I knew nothing about it. I think what you are achieving is amazing but don't do this again because I may not always be around to bail you out.'

Tip for success
Teach your child self-discipline.

There are a number of ways we can help our children to develop self-discipline but the primary one is by example. We don't want to set the example of 'do as I say not as I do' so we need to demonstrate self-discipline ourselves. It's not helpful for a child to witness her parent flying off the handle, 'out of control'. So take a deep breath and count to ten when you are fit to explode. Walk away from the scene of the crime and consider what your reaction should be. *Show* your child what self-discipline really is! On difficult days when I can't bring myself to break the feeling of anger, I imagine that this is our last day together. The effect is miraculous! It's amazing how that thought allows grace to seep through and helps you to see things in perspective.

Of course, self-discipline isn't only about controlling anger – it's about how we live every part of our life. It's the way we behave, the way we eat, the way we drink, the way we interact with others . . . and much more! This doesn't mean that as parents we have to be saints, with every reaction perfectly balanced, but it does mean we need to be realistic about the example we set for our children. Are we expecting our children to be better self-disciplined than we are ourselves? Are we showing our children the way we'd like them to behave?

Inevitably – and despite our best efforts – there will be occasions when our anger (even if it is justifiable) boils over. On these occasions we still need to make it clear that it's the action, not the child herself, that is unacceptable. (It's very easy in the heat of the moment to make our children feel that they are the worst creatures on the face of the earth.) Focus on what she's done rather than on the child herself. Say things like, 'I'm really angry with the mess you've made' rather than, 'You're a careless, useless child. I can't trust you with anything, can I?'

Sometimes, no matter how reasonable you think you have been, your child may get upset with you for telling her off. In two-parent families you may find a 'good cop, bad cop' situation (metaphorically speaking!), where one parent tells the child off and the child then goes to the other parent for a hug. The other parent can present a united front, explaining the situation in calmer terms to the child. The added bonus, too, is that it's not always you who has to be the baddie. As single parents, we have to be both lawmaker and peace broker – all at the same time. This is easier said than done – especially when we're emotionally worn out. Sometimes there is nothing we can do but stick to our guns until the episode blows over.

The reality of day-to-day life is that it can be incredibly hard, but don't be disheartened. If you've gone off the deep end about muddy footprints or spilt lemonade, just go back and say sorry. It helps children to see the struggles you go through and to know that you're human and don't get it right all the time.

Tip for success
Remember that there is no such thing as the perfect parent.

Consistency

Despite the obvious challenges of providing discipline as a single parent, the benefit is that our children hear only one clear voice. There are no contradictions. Occasionally, with the best will in the world, two-parent families are sometimes split over the way to handle a situation. And it's easy to lose the plot in the confusion. Children can easily learn to play one parent off against the other.

That said, it's really important that we are consistent in the way we discipline our children. It means being fair even when you've had a foul day at work, missed the train, forgotten to go shopping for tea and feel as if you're going down with the flu.

Regardless of how we feel from day to day, our children need to know where they stand with us. If we chop and change our approach from one day to the next they won't have a clue. We need to be consistent in our approach – we should work out how we will deal with bad behaviour and then stick to our plans. There will always be problems that we haven't planned for (children will always find new ways to surprise us!) so we need to have a general idea of how to deal with all sorts of unacceptable behaviour. Be prepared and then be consistent. Too tall an order? Maybe – but it's certainly something to aim for. And when we're inconsistent we must be prepared to say we've got it wrong.

Tip for success

Discipline needs to be consistent in order to really work.

Admitting mistakes

There is something terribly liberating about owning up. It helps to open up honest communication. As parents it shows we care enough about our children to apologise to them. Admitting mistakes also breaks down any potentially alienating barriers between parent and child (especially teenagers). They see us as more reasonable and that can only be a good thing!

Let's face it – no one likes a know-it-all (especially our children). If we're never wrong we'll seem too good to be true and run the risk of losing our children's respect. And if we're dishonest in our behaviour we give them the green light to be dishonest in their behaviour too.

I've got it wrong again!

When we admit our mistakes, we're asking for our children's forgiveness. Love and forgiveness allow failures to happen, and it can be a relief for children to know they have imperfect parents as (if my family is anything to go by!) parents certainly don't have perfect children.

I hate being in conflict with Justine especially when I know I'm in the wrong. Admitting my mistake goes a long way towards getting rid of that feeling of awfulness. However, it's amazing how jealously we parents hold onto our angry stance, even if it makes us feel wretched.

Love means . . . always having to say you're sorry

Saying sorry to our children and *really* meaning it can be one of the most powerful messages of love we can express. Apart from anything else it shows we're trying to be fair. And it shows that we are fallible too. Our children expect us to be just, and our injustice can lead to their discouragement. They also learn far more from how we behave than from what we tell them to do. If they experience us admitting our failures, they'll be far more likely to admit theirs, and it's much easier to grow and develop in a culture of grace and forgiveness, than one of blame and falsehood.

> ## Tip for success
> Success does not mean always getting it right – but it does mean acknowledging to our child, as well as ourselves, when we get it wrong.

Another advantage to admitting mistakes is that it gives us and our children an opportunity to sit down and really talk. When I'm in the wrong and feeling a bit sheepish, I make Justine's favourite dish of macaroni cheese (her favourite because it's the only dish I can make successfully!), followed by her favourite dessert: luxury vanilla ice cream. I unplug the telephone and use the mealtime, when we're relaxed and digging into the family-sized tub of ice cream, to apologise. These times can be difficult (it's never *easy* to apologise), filled with tears and laughter, but before we know it we're discussing all sorts of things – from the serious to the frivolous! I never fail to be amazed at just how much my teenager actually *wants* to talk to me, and I never fail to be amazed at just how utterly loving and forgiving she is.

YOU NEED TO APOLOGISE, BECAUSE IT'S AGES SINCE YOU DID ANYTHING WORTH APOLOGISING WITH ICE CREAM FOR...

Tip for success

Forgiveness should be the cornerstone of our relationship
with our children.

It's never too late

The hardest mistakes to admit, though, are the ones that we
know have really hurt our children. There are mistakes that may
have happened years ago, which with hindsight we know are
wrong but now seem impossible to put right. One of the scariest
aspects of parenting is knowing that there is no dress-rehearsal.
There is no opportunity to practise first before we jump in with
both feet. How many times have you heard someone say, 'If
only I could do it all again'? But the reality is we can't. What can
the majority of us do, when we don't realise that things are
going wrong until after the event? How can we deal with the
long-term hurts we've inflicted on our children?

Maybe we've done or said the wrong thing, or approached
something with the wrong attitude. I've definitely said things
that now, years later, wrench my heart with regret. It's important
to let our children know that we're sorry for the times we've
failed them, however long ago. We can explain that we did
what we thought was best at the time, but now, looking back
we realise our errors and are deeply sorry. It can be quite a
relief for them to know that we've acknowledged responsibility
in something that they might have been experiencing as not
only quite painful, but also unfair. Our admission helps to
unburden them. We should take care, though, that the situation
doesn't become counterproductive and we purge every detail.
Often, a simple acknowledgment of how things were will suffice.
You may be surprised how willing they are to forgive (though
sometimes it will take longer for them to forget). Our children
have an enormous capacity to love unconditionally – and they
want everything to be OK.

There may also be situations where your relationship with your child has broken down – seemingly of its own accord. You may feel that you are only partly to blame. Whatever the situation it's never too late to make a move and put things right. You don't need to apologise for things you haven't done but you can apologise for the things you have done wrong, however small. Any kind of olive branch, offered in the right attitude, can help to restore a relationship. Make sure you don't attach any conditions to your apology – it needs to be an unconditional one – then leave it to your child to respond.

- Without forgiveness, resentment builds up on both sides.
- Admitting mistakes releases the pressure valve, allowing both sides to heal – it helps to restore the relationship.
- Someone has to make the first move in a stalemate situation and, as the parent, we ought to be big enough to take that step, even if it's only a tiny one.

As with all parenting issues, how to succeed in the area of discipline is quite subjective. It will constantly involve us reassessing the way we view a situation, being prepared to change our 'lens'. We need to develop true communication by seeking to understand all aspects of the situation before we put our boundaries in place and have the courage that in placing such boundaries, we will be understood. We need to empower our children by acknowledging good and offering praise. We need to lead by example by being prepared to 'put it right when we get it wrong, and remember . . . *it's only too late if you don't start now!*

Discipline checklist

Check:

- The way we speak to our children.
- How we deliver our message.
- How often we praise our children.
- If we are fair with punishment.
- If our discipline is consistent.
- Our children's boundaries and the way that we've communicated them to our children.
- How often *we* say sorry.

5
You Are Not Alone
Support mechanisms

I can still remember the shock of realising how difficult it is to be a parent. When it first hit me, I looked around for support and advice from anyone who had children. I would snap up the first piece of advice to come my way, and then listen to different and possibly conflicting counsel. It must have had an awful effect on Justine. I lost confidence and seemed unable to make a decision for myself. Luckily at the time I had really good friends and my mum, who gave me solid advice. They spent a lot of time reassuring me I was OK and doing a good job. I don't know if I was or I wasn't but I did need my self-esteem building up.

Very few of us can manage to get through life on our own, as the words of the song suggest, 'we all need somebody to lean on', especially when it comes to parenting. *All* parents, not just single ones, need support and advice. None of us have all the answers or can do this on our own. We just haven't been made that way.

One of the problems is that the society in which we live often no longer functions in an interdependent way – we have lost our community spirit. There is a myth that tells us that success equals self-sufficiency – and it's a myth that is all around us: on the TV, on the radio, in newspapers and magazines. An increasingly popular song at funerals these days is 'My way' – which says it all! The myth is *far* from the truth but it reinforces the belief that we are failures if we can't manage everything alone. In reality, we really can't raise children on our own – we need help and support. What's more, our children need a variety of adults to interact with.

Build me up, buttercup...

It's my observation that one of the biggest problems for many single parents (myself included) is a loss of self-confidence and an inability to trust our own instincts. The danger, of course, is that in our quest to find the right advice, we end up relying on anyone who appears self-confident. We need to discern who gives good counsel instead of being tempted to listen to the loudest voice. Various friends have particular pearls of wisdom. Your mum might be the expert on chickenpox and toddler tantrums while a close friend with children the same age may be the one to consult on whether your child should go to a particular party. (Or whether your nine-year-old son is staying up too late despite the fact that he says all his friends are up until eleven o'clock.)

When we feel unsure about the decisions we are making, we may end up asking friends and family for advice. Some will give good advice and others might not. Whatever advice we receive, we're still the ones left with the dilemma of what to do. It's really important that we *trust our instincts*. At the end of the day, when we've sifted through the mountain of good advice we've collected, we need to sit down and ask ourselves what *we* really feel is the best choice or decision for our children. And then go with that. As parents, the ones who know our children best, we're the ones in the best position to make the decisions – we don't need to be swayed by persuasive voices if they go against our instincts. We should listen to what we really feel and stick with it.

I've been very fortunate in having supportive family and friends. And how I have needed them! For one thing, I didn't know what guilt was until I became a parent. Guilt doesn't just come with the placenta; it comes with the adoption papers too!

Tip for success

Listen to your instincts and constantly test them against your value system.

Smile and the world smiles with you . . .

If you're not in a supportive environment it's important that you make the most of any support which comes your way. Don't be afraid to say 'yes' if someone offers you some kind of help. If another parent at school offers to share school runs with you then try to work something out – that way not only will you be getting practical help but also you'll be building up new friendships. When your children are at primary school, for example, a lot of contacts come from meeting people at the school gate. The school gate is a hotbed of contacts – and of gossip! You may not be the only one who really needs friendship and support. There will be loads of parents like you – they just may not have the courage to show it. Someone else out there might be shy or lacking in confidence, so why not make the first move!

Try to develop new friendships:

- Start off by smiling at people – it works wonders as an icebreaker!

- Find out if there is anyone who could share the dropping off and collecting routines with you. Look out for people at the school gate, crèche or nursery door who might be travelling in your direction.
- Sometimes the best way to get support is to offer it. Helping someone out might be the first step you need to take to build up a network of help for yourself. As you develop relationships with people you should be able to support each other in all kinds of different ways.

Many parents find that it's their peer group that becomes their support network. Grandparents might not be as involved as they used to be – they're off leading their own lives or they may live too far away to offer practical help. So be realistic about where you look for help. Your local library or Citizens' Advice Bureau should have a list of groups for parents – useful if you're new to the area and have no idea where to start looking.

Tip for success

Making the first move is a good way to make new friends.

No man (or woman) is an island!

Traditional family and community structures have radically changed in recent decades (families are generally more nuclear than extended now), which means that there aren't always experienced family members on hand to help us out. When I was a child it wasn't unusual to be looked after by my next-door neighbours. In fact both our back doors were never closed. We were continually in and out of each other's houses. If I came home from school and my mum wasn't in, I'd just go next door and have my tea there. We didn't need an official arrangement and we didn't even consider it as a form of childminding. I wasn't a 'latchkey kid' – it was just the way we shared.

Nowadays, families are spread across the country, if not the world – we often feel as if we live in a global community rather than a local one. The problem is that you can't call your mum to help you with the baby if she's living in Australia. Or you may have moved to a new area, only to discover that you end up knowing no one other than the postman and the person who turns up on your doorstep selling dusters. Whoever you are, whatever your circumstance, whether you're the landowner with nannies and a four-wheel drive and children in public school or living in an inner-city estate, you may feel isolated.

So what do you do? First, make a list of the networks of people that you *do* have contact with. This might be work, neighbours, parents from your child's school, friends who live nearby, family, etc. Then think about the individuals within each of those networks who you could make an effort to see more often, and this might be enough to get you started.

1. People like us

Organisations such as Gingerbread offer formal support for single-parent families through a network of self-help groups. There are approximately 160 local Gingerbread groups in England and Wales that are all run on a self-help basis, by single parents elected from the membership. Each local group aims to provide a meeting place for both parents and children as well as a practical and emotional support network. Each Gingerbread group caters for the needs of its members so each group varies from area to area. Gingerbread's details can be found at the back of this book.

Find out if there are any single-parent groups meeting in your area by asking at your local library or your GP's surgery. I've met countless single parents who have found that the support, care and empathy they receive from organisations like Gingerbread are excellent and empowering – helping them to feel they've got their social life back. You'll meet other parents who may be in very similar situations to you and will understand your needs. And there's no reason why you can't become

involved in both single-parent groups and other social groups –
you may have to cut your cloth accordingly and only attend one
type of meeting a week but it will broaden your interests and
your friendships.

2. Explore new horizons

We can become so involved with our children that we virtually
lose touch with the outside world and getting 'back out there'
can seem like attempting to climb a very difficult mountain. Yet
single-parenting needn't be a life sentence to single living. We all
need friends and, though it might not always seem like it, there
are lots of opportunities to make new friends with similar interests.

There are also a wide variety of groups with which you can
become involved. What you choose to get involved with will
depend on what interests you and the time you have available
to you:

- Check out your local paper for nearby groups or meetings that appeal to you.
- Find out about evening or day classes – some will provide a crèche.
- If your child is school age get involved with the parents association.
- Go to your local library and ask for a list of local groups.
- Listen to your local radio station to see if there are any events run by local groups that you'd like to go to.
- Find out if you have a community centre in your area – and if so, find out what sort of groups meet there.

Tip for success

Be bold enough to look for groups of people with the same interests as you.

Don't be disheartened if you can't find a network that suits you straight away – keep looking. Think about what your interests are and then arrange some childcare – either a friend or a crèche – and meet with similar people who share common ground and won't want to talk about children all the time.

Think about the interests that you pursued before you became a parent. Ask yourself, 'If I was to find myself now with no friends, no social structures, what would I do? Where would I go?'

You can go as far as sitting down and making a list of all the things you like doing – you may be surprised by your list! And then go out and do one of those things whether it's lace-making or swimming, baking or football. In the end it doesn't really matter what we choose to do because wherever we go we're guaranteed to meet other people. We may very well even stumble across someone in a similar position, with similar needs. They may also need someone to share the childcare or a shoulder to cry on, or simply someone to have fun with!

Tip for success
Don't neglect yourself – try to make time to
pursue your interests.

I took up a life-drawing class at the local further education college. It took a bit of organising, as far as baby-sitters for Justine were concerned, but I went ahead and did it anyway. People attended it from all walks of life, including a handful of parents (thanks to the crèche facilities for very small children). Over time the group became quite friendly and it wasn't unusual for a bunch of us to go for a coffee after class. I found the experience totally refreshing, and I developed a new talent.

If you're really unsure about going into a new group for the first time – whether it's to a local sports centre or to a local debating society – arrange to take a friend with you so you don't have to actually walk in on your own. You'd think that with doing the sort of job I do, meeting new people and entering new situations would be a piece of cake. Well, far from it. Even I have to take a deep breath and be courageous when confronting new situations.

3. Expect the unexpected

Your social groups will almost certainly change as your child grows up so be prepared to be flexible; you never know where possibilities are lurking. There is a lovely line in the seventeenth-century nun's prayer that says: 'Teach me, O Lord, to recognise unexpected opportunities in unexpected places and unexpected gifts in unexpected people.'

Sometimes we make friends in the most unexpected places. You could start up a conversation at a bus stop and end up making a lifelong friend! It does happen. And how many friendships have developed because of a chance encounter? We need to always be on the lookout to meet new people and make new friends. The more open we are to those sorts of possibilities, the more likely we are to find friends and the value of such friendships is inestimable.

As single parents we can easily catch ourselves thinking, 'What am I doing wrong?' Then through a timely conversation we discover that we're not doing anything wrong – that's just the way it is. Looking at other people's situations can help us take a fresh look at our own. A friend of mine has five children – all completely different. To me, she's a kind of supermum. But through talking to her I realise that she has the same concerns and worries as me and, as a result, I feel affirmed as a single parent that what I'm doing is actually OK.

Friendships like these don't happen overnight but it only takes a few minutes to sow the seeds.

Doctor, doctor

Apart from informal support networks, we can also call on the assistance of professionals for advice about healthcare – particularly concerning preschool children.

Midwives

We all dip in and out of healthcare services throughout our entire lives – they are there to help us and we should make the most of them. As a parent, the first person to offer care to you and your new baby is the community midwife. She is responsible for a new mum and her baby for the first twenty-eight days. She'll call in on you every day to begin with and then will be on hand if you need advice over the first four weeks.

Health visitors

If there is something that you're worried about and your child is under five, one possible option is to go and speak to your health visitor. Health visitors are usually attached to GP surgeries and are there to take over when the mother is discharged by the midwife. They should be able to give you advice about your child's health and development from nought to five years old and cover subjects such as:

- Whether your child is putting on enough weight and growing properly
- Whether your child is developing properly
- How to deal with common illnesses
- When to get your child vaccinated
- How to encourage your child to eat properly
- How to make your home safe for a young child
- How to cope with difficulties such as a child who doesn't sleep
- How to cope with teething problems
- Where to find local nurseries, parent and toddler groups and childminders.

Health visitors should also be able to give you contact details for other sources of help. A health visitor comes into contact with hundreds of different people and as many problems, so she should be well qualified in pointing you in the right direction.

Community practitioners

Never forget that your GP is only a phone call away! If your child has a particular and urgent health problem get in contact with your doctor. For the less urgent, or if you're really exhausted and struggling, make an appointment to see your doctor. Many doctors are sympathetic to the stress and strain of being a single parent and will be able to point you in the right direction for further help if that's what you need.

If you're nervous or worried about speaking to your health visitor or another professional, or sense they're not on the same wavelength as you (and it does happen), take a friend along with you. There are times when, no matter how articulate or confident we are, we feel intimidated and vulnerable so it's good to have somebody along for moral support.

It might also be useful to make notes before you go and while you're there. It's very easy to walk out of the consulting room and realise that you have completely forgotten the advice you've been given! No one should mind you jotting down the stuff you need to remember.

Pharmacists

Pharmacists are probably the most local of all the healthcare professionals and we don't use them enough! There's bound to be a pharmacy not far from you and you can always give them a ring if you're indoors with a sick child. Pharmacists are well qualified to deal with most of the minor ailments we are faced with as parents. And they have many of the solutions at their fingertips. Pharmacists are a mine of information as well as providing leaflets about a whole range of conditions and problems.

Tip for success
Don't be afraid to make the most of the professional services available to you.

Helplines

In addition to your GP you can also make use of NHS Direct. This is a helpline answered by nurses. If you or your child has a medical problem and you need further advice you can give them a ring. Be ready to answer questions about your own or your child's condition – the helpline staff will reassure you and tell you what you need to do. Details are at the back of this book.

Parentline Plus is another helpline – this one is aimed specifically at parents. You can ring them with any kind of non-medical problem and they should be able to offer you advice or give you the number of someone who can.

There are many other statutory and voluntary organisations who provide help and information for parents. While we can't list them all check out the back of the book for further details.

6
Who's Holding the Baby?

Childcare issues

I can't count the number of magazine and newspaper interviews I've given where I've been asked, 'How on earth do you manage childcare?' It occurred to me a long time ago how fortunate I have always been to have my family – particularly my mum – to step into the breech with Justine whenever I've needed her to. But that doesn't mean to say that I haven't struggled from time to time and felt those feelings of guilt, confusion and conflict that childcare issues can create. After all, which of us has not been faced with the conflicting demands of a job and a family; or of a sick child (whether genuine or otherwise) who doesn't want to go to school, even though we're due at work in an hour; or the weight of responsibility of making the important decisions about childcare with no partner to refer to?

The reality for many single parents, however, is that the pressing issue of childcare is a day-to-day one. You may feel that you have no option but to hold down a job in order to put bread on the table and to provide a bit of sanity for yourself. In these circumstances, good childcare is an absolute necessity.

Fifty ways to leave your ...

There are a million and one occasions when we need to leave our children in the care of someone else. The reasons will vary from pleasure to arduous work. From short, infrequent trips to regular, long, daily commitments. Whatever the situation, we need to make careful, informed choices as to whom we leave 'in charge'. Talking to many single parents – and parents generally – I have realised that establishing a successful childcare set-up is often an agonising series of decisions which, like most things, will have to be constantly reassessed as we, our children and our needs change. But be comforted. I know few parents – particularly mums – who don't feel if only the very smallest tug at their heart when they have to leave their children, even for the more pleasurable activities of life. And the vast majority of children that that I know of, once settled into a good routine, have been happy and contented with their carers – growing in confidence and making friends easily with their childminder and their peers.

WERE THERE ANY TEARS ON YOUR FIRST DAY AT NURSERY?

YES – BUT DAD SOON CHEERED UP ...

Tip for success
Don't always think it's bad to leave your child.

My friend Rachael runs a playgroup. She says, 'When new children start at playgroup, I always know the ones who are used to having even a short time away from mum or dad. They are generally the most secure. They know their carers are going to come back at 12.30 to pick them up.'

If you leave your child in someone else's care for a short while from when they're young both of you will get used to the idea – it won't be so traumatic when you drop her off at playgroup or at the childminder's for the first time. Your child will be more confident that you will return and you will be more secure about leaving her.

Nose to the grindstone

The numbers of women entering the labour market has increased dramatically over the last fifteen years. In Britain, 49 per cent of mothers go back to paid work before their babies reach their first birthdays. Whether you're a working mum or dad, one thing is certain: sorting out childcare will be one of your main priorities.

If you're looking for childcare for the first time or if you're looking to change your current childcare situation the most important thing for you to remember is to *trust your instincts*. To put it another way, choose only childcare that you are *really* happy with. This small sentence really can't be emphasised enough. Don't add to your existing stress by worrying excessively about how your child is when you are not with them because you're not confident about the care that they may be receiving. A nursery or childminder might have good recommendations/references coming out of their ears but if you don't feel it's the right place for your child don't hesitate to find somewhere else. Children and their needs vary and at the end of the day you know your child and what she needs better than anyone, so it's important that you are both comfortable with the arrangements.

Tip for success
When it comes to childcare – trust your instincts.
Only go with it if you're happy.

Louise is a single mum, having separated from her partner several years ago. She's found that society has changed a great deal from when she had her first baby:

When I first got married, women went back to work, after their children were born, to earn pin money, to get the added bits or to pay for the foreign holiday – but because of the way society has changed women have to work to pay the mortgage, to have the computer in the home (and as parents of secondary school children at least will tell you, the PC is almost becoming a necessity). Now we're not talking poverty or affluence, we're talking about fairly average, normal, everyday people. When it comes to having to go out to work – the reality – you have no choice but to put contingency plans for childcare into place.

You will find that you have a variety of different childcare options. Some will suit you better than others and some will suit you better at different times in your child's life. Whatever you decide to do to begin with does not have to be set in stone – you can change according to your circumstances and your child's needs.

What follows is a list of options that you may wish to consider for your situation. If you have access to the Internet, you can find more information on each in the At Work section of the Parentalk website – www.parentalk.co.uk. There you will also find details of agencies and organisations that can assist you in determining your options, benefits to which you may be entitled and the current regulations for carers. Alternatively, you may wish to take a look at another book in this series – *How to Succeed as a Working Parent*, written by Steve Chalke – which tackles the whole work-family balance issue in more depth.

Childminders

If you have family members who are willing to look after your child – whether it be for a full working day or to give you the odd break – then you're in a great position. If you know the person who is caring for your child and particularly if they love your child, you will feel much happier about leaving her. If you're not so fortunate you'll need to look further afield.

Childminding is the most popular form of childcare. If you don't know of any registered childminders, get in touch with your local authority – they should have a list of childminders in your area. If you have children at school you may hear, through the grapevine, of mums and dads who are childminding – some schools even advertise names on their newsletters. Network wherever you can – the more friends and contacts you have, the more likely you are to pick up useful tips about local childminders. It's helpful if you have recommendations from friends to start with; otherwise it's a case of ringing round and meeting some likely childminders so that you can find one who you can work with and are happy with.

Registered childminders must be checked by the local authority. Their homes will have been inspected to make sure there are no obvious safety issues and they will have been checked themselves. A registered childminder will be allowed a limited number of children to look after – no more than three nought- to five-year-olds and three five- to eight-year-olds (including the childminder's own children).

Tip for success
The grapevine is a good source of information about potential childminders.

When choosing a childminder be prepared to make a lot of phone calls! It'll save you a great deal of time if you have a list of questions to ask and a list of information to give. Tell the childminder the age of your child or children and the date when you would need them to start. Ask the childminder how many children he or she looks after and if there are any pets in the house – you don't want to waste time visiting a childminder with two Alsatians if your two-year-old is terrified of dogs. Find out what the fees are before you arrange to go round – that way you'll know if this particular childminder is a viable option.

Arrange to see the childminder so you can find out if you're happy with each other. Take a friend or relative along for a second opinion – it's always good to have someone to talk the visit over with afterwards. Try to visit during the day so that you can see your childminder 'in action' with any other children they look after. Don't be afraid to ask questions and if there's something you forget to ask, ring. At the end of the day it's *your* child the childminder is looking after so you're entitled to ask as many relevant questions as you want. Bear in mind the following suggestions:

1. On a visit to a prospective childminder be honest about the hours you work and find out if they can be flexible if you have to be. Don't tell your childminder that you'll pick up your child every day at 5.30 p.m. if the reality is that you won't be able to get there until 6 p.m. – you'll only end up creating bad feelings between you. It's far better that you have an open, honest relationship from day one.

2. If you're visiting a prospective childminder on your own and you're worried that there are things you'll forget to ask, take a list of questions with you – work them out beforehand. It's really easy to let the obvious slip straight out of your mind when you're faced with a new situation on your own.

3. Remember to ask questions about food and mealtimes. Do the fees include lunch and tea? What sort of meals does the childminder give the children? You will also need to ask about toilet training if your child is still in nappies.

4. Develop a good relationship with your childminder before you leave your child and go off to work – this can't be stressed enough. You need to be really happy that your

child is being well looked after and you need to trust the person you're leaving her with. You won't be able to get to this point in one meeting. Take your child to meet your childminder, leave them together for a couple of hours as a 'dummy run'. If you can fit in a few of these that's better still. When your child comes home with a smile on her face, you'll relax!

5. It's a good idea to agree with your childminder potentially difficult issues before you begin. Find out what your childminder's views are on discipline. Your child needs consistency in her life and you need to be happy with the way the childminder deals with her. Ideally, choose a childminder who has a similar approach and attitude to life as you.

6. If you're going to be late or you have an after-work appointment give your childminder as much warning as possible. There are times when we are unavoidably held up but if you know you have to work late do check that your childminder is also happy to work extra hours – and do pay for that time.

7. Ask about holiday plans so you are not left high and dry at too short notice and, by the same token, keep your childminder fully informed of your plans. Ask your childminder to give you as much notice as possible regarding holidays, as you will want to have time to make alternative arrangements. And it's only fair that you do the same in return.

8. Don't look at your childminder as a rival for your child's affection but rather see them as on your side, part of the team involved in looking after your child – after all, you can't do it completely on your own.

9. Try to sort out as many of the minor issues as you can before they arise. For example, what does your child call your childminder? It may not seem to be an issue when you hand over your six-month-old baby but if your

eighteen-month-old calls her childminder Mummy or Daddy you may not feel so impressed!

Childminders are a good choice if you have more than one child to look after as they may well take siblings together – they are a good choice if you would prefer your child to be looked after in a home environment rather than in a nursery. They are also a good choice if you have school-age children who need a few hours of childcare at each end of the school day. Registered childminders who are also parents at your child's school are frequently the best choice as, chances are, you will already know them and they won't be expected in two places at 3.30 p.m. every day.

Nurseries

There are two kinds of nurseries – day nurseries where children are cared for during your working day and private nurseries which tend to run during school hours. They are two very different beasts! One thing you can be sure of with a nursery is that your child will get plenty of social interaction and she will mix with children of a similar age.

Like childminders, nurseries have to be registered so check with your local authority for a list. You may well find that some are popular and have waiting lists so start looking around as soon as possible.

Day nurseries will look after children from six weeks old to school age. They are run by a whole host of different organisations from the local council to the private owner. Some larger businesses may even provide day nurseries for their staff. Regardless of how they are run they will all have to undergo regular inspections and will have to comply with OFSTED standards. Generally speaking, this kind of nursery will open from 8 a.m. to 6 p.m. – giving you time to get to and from work. If you can find a suitable nursery near your workplace you will have less rushing around to do. As with childminders, do phone first with initial questions about whether there is a vacancy and how much the nursery charges. Phone calls will save you a lot of time and you can narrow the choice down to just a few possibilities.

Again, if you can, take a friend with you to have a look round. If not, make sure you are clear about the things you need to find out. Make a list of questions! Don't rush into making a decision, sleep on it and make sure you are totally happy with a nursery before committing your child into its care.

There are (current at time of writing) guidelines for staff/child ratios:

- One carer to three children for the under-twos
- One carer to four children for two- to three-year-olds
- One carer to eight children for three- to five-year-olds.

When you visit the nursery don't be afraid to ask questions!

- Find out what kinds of activities are available to the children. A good nursery will have a wide range of activities from 'messy' play (sand, water, clay and paint) to a quiet area where a child can sit and look at books. There should also be activity toys, such as tricycles, seesaws and possibly climbing frames, and games and toys that stimulate a child's imagination (dressing-up clothes).

- Is there an outdoor area? And what sort of toys does it have?
- Do the children go out on trips to places like the local library?
- Take your child along and see how she settles.
- Do *you* feel comfortable with the nursery? What's your first impression? Is it a friendly, clean environment?
- Find out about the nursery's policy on discipline.
- If your child is having meals there, ask to see a typical menu.
- Find out how flexible the nursery will be if you're running late.
- Make sure you know who to talk to if your child has a problem. Asking questions at the beginning can save you a lot of misunderstandings later on.

Tip for success
When visiting childminders or nurseries you can never ask too many questions!

Private nurseries take children who are out of nappies from about two and a half to school age. They are open the same hours as schools and during term-time. Most offer mornings or afternoons rather than whole days. Private nurseries prepare your child for 'real' school with a build-up of structured activities and are great if you can fit work into the few hours that your child is away.

If you know other parents who are also doing the nursery run you may be able to share lifts, which will give you extra working time. And as with childminders, talk to other parents and find out if they have been happy with the nursery care offered – the grapevine is a good source of information!

Similar to nurseries are playgroups and preschool groups. They have the same advantages and disadvantages as private nurseries when it comes to the hours they offer – if you don't work then it will be less of a problem. They are also OFSTED inspected and must be run by trained leaders. The popular preschool groups fill up quickly so you may have to put your child's name down for a particular group while she's still a baby – a bit like putting your child's name down for Eton as soon as he's born! It's never too early to start looking round.

Nannies

Nannies are more common than they used to be, (though none of them look like Mary Poppins!) but they are still very much the preserve of the more wealthy among us. A nanny will look after your child in your house and will quite possibly live in. If you work erratic or unpredictable hours and can afford one, a nanny is a good idea – but bear in mind that a nanny is probably the most expensive childcare option. Generally, nannies aren't inspected by OFSTED and they don't have to have childcare qualifications – although many will have. If you want to check out what kind of relevant qualifications a nanny might have contact CACHE (Council for Awards in Childcare Education) at 8 Chequer Street, St Albans, Herts, AL1 3XZ. In any case it's wise to take up references.

Your first place to look for a nanny might be at a local college where they run childcare courses or you could try a specialist agency. Again, don't be afraid of asking questions.

- Find out what experience the prospective nanny has with children and what it is that appeals to her about the job.
- Ask whether the nanny is prepared to live in/out – according to your need.

- Is she happy to baby-sit in the evenings and if so how often?
- Can she drive?
- If you're a non-smoker ask if she smokes.

It's important that you tie up details such as holiday pay, sick pay and how many hours you expect your nanny to work before she begins. You should all be clear about what is expected of each other before you enter into any formal agreement. There's no guarantee that nannies will stick with you on a long-term basis – they may be young and move on to higher education or pastures new, so you will have to be prepared to chop and change where necessary.

As with all employment, you should offer a letter of agreement or a written contract. If you employ a nanny through an agency they should be able to help you sort this out. Other things you need to be aware of are income tax – which you may have to deduct at source – and national insurance contributions. If you are not sure what to do or how to go about it get advice from your tax office. It's always better to ask than bury your head in the sand and hope for the best!

After-school clubs

With so many parents working, after-school clubs are springing up all over the place – it shouldn't be too difficult to find one near you. If you have school-age children and you work a full day, your options will be limited to childminders or one of these clubs. Some operate on school premises; others can be found in community centres. Like nurseries, they are regularly inspected by OFSTED so there should be information available about each club for you to look at. Go and have a look at one and take your child – see if she's happy with the set-up; after all she'll be spending a few hours there every day.

It's good to talk

Whatever your choice of childcare, talk to parents who have been to the same nurseries/childminders/after-school clubs and find out about their experiences. It's really important to pick up local pieces of information – good and bad – about your particular choice of childcare so that you can make the best choice for your child. Remember what suits one child may not suit another. And whoever you choose to look after your child, make time to talk to them and find out how your child is getting on. It's so easy to get into the habit of rushing around so that you drop off your child and pick her up without spending any time with her carers. You don't just want them to approach you with problems; you want to talk to them about the good things that are happening with your child as well.

Tip for success

Make time to talk to the people who care for your child.

Always keep in mind the fact that childcare is no substitute for your care – it is complementary care. When you are with your child make the most of the time you have together. However well your child may be looked after, you will still be Number One in her life – at least for a few years!

This is not the way I planned it

If your childcare plans don't work out the way you hoped, then don't be afraid to make changes. If you're not happy with your childminder or nursery or if they're not happy with the hours you are expecting from them, then talk to them. Tell the person who is looking after your child that you have some things you would like to discuss and make an appointment – act in a professional manner.

Avoid rushing in at the end of a long day in a steaming rage

– plan out what you intend to say before you get there and be very clear about the problem as you see it. Neither should you make wild accusations. Your aim should be to talk things over in a way that is productive. If your childcarer wants to see you about something – take a calm approach and admit your mistakes if it's you who's not keeping to the agreement. It may be that adjustments can be made on either side – but if not then think about other options. If you're really not happy with some aspect of your child's care you will definitely need to move your child – but check out where you stand legally before you do anything rash – you may have to give notice or pay fees until the end of the month or longer.

Tip for success

If you're concerned about the care your child is receiving, trust your instincts, talk things over with a close friend – then act.

Back-ups

Whatever we decide to do, we need to have a back-up plan – at least one and preferably as many as we can make hang together. We never know what's round the corner – children get sick, childminders get sick, mums and dads get sick and we don't want to be left in the lurch. The more people we have to support us, the easier we will find it. It's better to sort out our back-ups before we need them – that way we'll feel less anxious about any potential problems.

- If you have a childminder then find out if they have a back-up registered childminder in case of sickness.
- Find out your employer's view of you taking time off to look after a sick child *before* it happens.
- Make a list of friends or family who are willing and able to look after your child at short notice.

However well we are organised there are days when it will all go wrong. You may well feel that you're in the wrong place, doing the wrong thing, if your child is ill and being looked after by a friend and you are at work. It's important that you take a broad view and recognise that you are doing the best for your child – even on the days when it doesn't feel that way. If you have older children you will, at least, be able to talk to them and explain why you can't necessarily always take time off work when they are ill.

You may also feel bad about having to ask for favours all the time – or at least it may feel like all the time – from the same people. The reality is that none of us can manage all of the demands of bringing up children on our own – not even the most dedicated parent. If you have people around you who are willing to support you, then you need to take that support. It may well be that somewhere down the line you'll be able to help another parent who is struggling on their own. So remember that however difficult a patch you may be going through at the moment, it will get better. Children don't stay young and dependent for ever and there is light at the end of the tunnel, as far as baby-sitting favours forever are concerned.

Tip for success

Try to remember that you won't be asking for baby-sitting favours for the rest of your life.

Home alone?

All parents have to make the decision as to when their child is old enough to be left at home alone. Your child must be able and responsible enough to look after themselves and that will vary from child to child. At the end of the day no parent wants a disaster on their hands so most will think carefully before they leave a child on her own, even for the odd half-hour. Build up the time you leave your child alone when she is ready – and

LOOK MUM, I KNOW YOU DON'T WANT TO LEAVE ME HOME ALONE BUT I DON'T THINK BEING IN MY WENDY HOUSE COUNTS.

make sure she knows who to contact/what to do in an emergency.

If you want an evening out – something that most single parents need but find hard to arrange – always choose a baby-sitter who is over sixteen and someone you know. Having said that, there are some sixteen-year-olds who might not be responsible enough to look after your baby/young child and some fifteen-year-olds who would be fantastic, so you will have to judge their suitability. See if you can team up with other parents in a baby-sitting circle whereby you all baby-sit for each other. Networking is the key so that you don't feel alone, especially if you haven't got doting grandparents or aunties and uncles to hand.

Some single parents sacrifice evenings out in order to provide structured/consistent bedtimes for their children. Tracy's husband left her when her daughter was three months old. Although Tracy had a supportive family she made the decision to stay at home every evening with her daughter until the child was two years old. In practice, this meant that Tracy was there to settle her daughter whenever she woke up, but it also meant Tracy spent hundreds of evenings sitting at home on her own with no other adult to talk to. Tracy doesn't regret any of the evenings she spent on her own, although she found it hard – it was a sacrifice she was prepared to make.

Things can get tricky when we have teenagers who are too young to be left alone but too old to be 'baby-sat'. We have to continually adjust and work out how to adapt to the changing needs of growing children. Childcare gets easier . . . then it gets harder again before our children finally leave home.

Jackie is a single mum with three children. She says this:

I don't really like going out in the evenings – I'd rather be there for my kids but thank God for mobile phones when I do go out! I can stay in touch with my children wherever they are – and they can always get hold of me. I know my children would love me to be at home cooking, fixing the cupboards, doing nothing. They like me to be around so they can ignore me sometimes!

However old our children are, they will probably want us around in the evenings. Occasionally, we may have to plead our case to be let out! Everyone has to make their own decision about how much they leave their child in the care of others. All parents need a break from continuous childcare, very particularly single parents, so we shouldn't be afraid to take time out if that's what we need. We should make sure that our children are in safe hands and then . . . relax!

7
Juggling Time and Money

Resources

I'm blessed with many odd and 'useful' talents – juggling is one of them! I learned to juggle at a circus skills workshop for Blue Peter *many years ago – no surprise there! I still remember the agonising hours of witnessing the reality of juggling (i.e. the teacher's success) versus the impossibility (my failure). My brain just couldn't compute the skill of keeping three balls in the air using one pair of hands!*

For many single parents, balancing work and family can often feel like that. But unlike the juggling workshop, where I could admit defeat and walk away, single parents don't have that luxury. We have to find a solution. By the way (as a word of encouragement) I finally mastered the juggling . . .

The majority of parents feel as if they are being continually stretched in terms of emotions, time and money. Single parents probably have to stretch everything that little bit further – and on their own. There is never enough time to do what we have to do and there is never enough money to do it. We feel as if we are running to stand still and all the time we're doing that we're trying to be a good parent – no wonder we feel exhausted!

It seems that once we have children we spend so much of our time absorbed in providing for them that it's easy to forget *why* we wanted them in the first place. When my friend Trevor's wife died eighteen months ago he became acutely aware of his daughter's needs. Overnight he became the main breadwinner and primary carer. Overnight he had to sell his shares in his company and apply for family credit because he was no longer able to work the demanding hours expected by his partners. Although desperately struggling to make ends meet he still he believes he's made the right decision.

Keeping your eye on the ball

So how do we keep all our juggling balls in the air? How do we manage to be all we need to be and do all we need to do? The key to juggling is in the timing and keeping that all-important 'eye on the ball'. It's so easy in life to get the 'timing' wrong – to be distracted from our goals. Very few of us mean to put the demands of our work before the demands of our children but it can happen without us even realising. It creeps upon us and we don't even notice.

As most single parents will probably be both homemaker and main breadwinner we need to carefully consider the effects of work, both positive and negative, on our home situation. Of course the ideal is to find a balance.

If we're struggling just to survive on benefit it may not be practical to be a full-time stay-at-home parent – even if we strongly believe our children need us there. Similarly it's no good fooling ourselves that by working every waking hour in order to give our children the latest outfit or gadget but never seeing or spending time with them, we are any nearer perfection.

The truth is that we all have *our own* bottom line – our point of no compromise. Some of us may consider it vital to be home when our children get in from school. For others, bedtime may well be sacred. We might, however, decide that the extra hours of work really are necessary to provide that much-sought-after pair of trainers (and a bit of sanity!).

Under pressure

It's really worth spending a few minutes of our hard-earned spare time to work out if there is any way we can ease the pressure. The first step is to assess what we're trying to achieve and what we, and our children, actually need in terms of time and money. However we become single parents, it's vital that we are realistic in assessing our family's needs. It's just as important for us to take a long, cool look at our financial situation, as it is for us to understand the value of family relationships – recognising that part of our children's needs includes our physical presence. At this point it's not so much about juggling as preparing to walk the tightrope! I don't know much about tightrope walking (and no, I haven't tried that!) but I do know that finding your point of balance is the *key* to staying on the rope! Everyone's balance point is slightly different but in order for it to be maintained we will need to keep making constant, minor adjustments.

Having the ability to tightrope walk and juggle isn't unique to single parents. Actually all parents need to learn these skills. We can all have the courage to re-evaluate what our needs and the needs of our children really are. Perhaps our circumstances force those of us who are single parents to learn these skills more quickly. So, as we're in a position to lead the way, let's be trail-blazers!!

We need to ask ourselves:

- What is our role as parents?
- What are our priorities?
- What do our children need in terms of time?
- What do our children need in terms of money?

If your children are old enough you might want to include them in this 'appraisal'. What do they see as important? Once you have worked out what you have to do, you can then get yourself organised. Prioritise the things that you have to do, then work out a rota for everything else. This means, in reality, that if many of the domestic jobs are done less often in favour of you spending time with your child – so be it. Practically speaking, if your children are young you will have less choice than if you're a parent to an older child or teenager. Do what's essential regularly – cooking and washing – and do the less essential – dusting and vacuuming – every now and then. If you have older children, work out a rota so that everyone pulls their weight and you don't get left with everything on top of working and looking after them. The more organised you can be the further your time will go as you won't waste it doing things which are unnecessary.

Tip for success
Once you know what you are trying to achieve you have a better chance of achieving it.

In my situation, the more I worked, the more money I needed to sustain the lifestyle. As family time was continually squeezed by work commitments, I'd choose takeaways or eating out as preferred alternatives to cooking. I'd travel by taxi in favour of public transport; I'd pay for childcare, house-cleaning, ironing – whatever was needed. I was also spending more on household repairs and builders – even more at the supermarket – just because I had little time to shop around.

I had created a very expensive lifestyle simply because I hadn't balanced my time properly between home and work. Eventually I reached the point where both work and family life were on the brink of suffering. Changes had to be made. I took the opportunity to re-evaluate and re-prioritise the way I spent my time and money. It wasn't easy at the time but looking back I'm so pleased I did it.

Wherever you are ... *be there*!

I love my work and I can't begin to tell you the number of times I have struggled to put the pressures of motherhood to one side while I get on with the job in hand. One of my worst moments was when Justine was actually with me . . . I was presenting live from Heathrow Airport for BBC Children in Need. Justine was enjoying watching from the sidelines. Suddenly, from the corner of my eye I saw her collapse. She had passed out right in the middle of my live link. There was simply nothing I could do. I had to focus on the next two minutes of my live link and leave her in the capable hands of my PA! I'm pleased to say that everything turned out fine in the end. Justine recovered fully but it took a little longer for me to get over it.

I'll admit, few of us have to literally live out the lines of 'the show must go on' but there is something very beneficial in being focused on what needs to be done. When we're at work it's important that we *are* at work in body and mind! That way we can give our best, whatever we are doing, and that in turn will lead to much greater personal fulfilment. Equally, when we are with our children it's vital that *we are* with them – 100 per cent. I often used to come home from work preoccupied with the day's events or too exhausted and unable to give or get anything from my time with Justine.

Tip for success
Time is more precious to children than money.

I learned this lesson the hard way. I was so absorbed in what I needed to do *for* Justine, I overlooked the most important thing, which was *being* with her.

Making the most of it

There are times when our work hours do change and there's little we can do about it. We may have to suddenly work longer hours than normal or it may be that we're under pressure at work and take the stress and worry home with us. It's easy to feel that you're never really there – your mind is still running through lists of figures or problem-solving. What we need to do, however, regardless of our work commitments, is to make the most of the time we do have with our children. If you've been through a difficult, time-consuming patch at work, make an extra special effort to spend time with your child when you do get home – even if it means putting other commitments on the back burner for a while. When we are at home we should:

- Do our best to switch off from work.
- Leave work worries where they belong – at work.
- Concentrate on what we're doing at home and who we're with.
- Try, at least, to be aware of when work is spilling over into family life and, to an extent, vice versa.
- Ask ourselves this question: If this was my child's last day or my last day on earth, how would I spend my time?
- Remember this . . . No one ever lay on their deathbed wishing they'd spent more time in the office!

I have had constantly to re-evaluate my role as sole parent – I have had to consciously weigh up the demands of home and work. For me, as with many other parents, home life has the edge but, however we look at it, money and time are inextricably linked. By trimming our finances and stretching our time some of the burdens of being a single parent have undoubtedly eased, but in their place are new challenges – we're still walking the tightrope.

DAD! I WISH YOU'D STOP BRINGING YOUR WORK HOME WITH YOU!

MUSEUM CURATOR

Money

In Britain there are nearly two million single parents, and there is no doubt in my mind that for most of us our children are our top priority. However, with over half of us living on less than £150 a week, and more than 50 per cent of us in debt, money is a major concern for all single parents.

A lack of money can make us feel powerless, especially if we're struggling to provide even the basics. This can be compounded when we constantly have to say 'no' to the things our children ask for. It's difficult not to compare ourselves with others but doing so, especially with those who are financially more stable than us, can lead to feelings of inadequacy. But having lots of money and being a great parent don't necessarily go hand in hand!

Tip for success

Money is a tool to be used – it's not an end in itself.

Weaving our way through the minefield of money issues is a tricky task. But whether we are trying to manage on benefit, or have significantly more income at our disposal, there is a common bond that unites us all – essentially, we are the sole providers for our family. This can be an awesome responsibility and particularly difficult if it has been imposed upon us though the death of a spouse or a relationship break-up. I don't know anyone who hasn't experienced a drop in their living standards after a relationship has broken down, and often the changes are dramatic.

Mike is a single dad who has struggled a great deal since his wife died. Juggling work and family has proved really difficult along with the financial worries he has had to face.

My wife Sally was uninsurable – she had a genetic disease, which meant that her life expectancy was only twenty-six. When we bought a house all the life insurances were in my name. When she died, there was therefore no money to come from insurance policies and, on top of that, there was a massive drop in our income due to the fact that we had been receiving so much from her invalidity benefits. I know it sounds daft but I wasn't aware of how much she had received. It turned out to be around £600 a month and that was immediately taken away from us. I still had to pay the mortgage and all the bills I had before. There was no change in that at all.

At that point, I wasn't paying for childminders. I did have to start sending Cassy to after-school clubs. I was very lucky that I found one in my local area that only charged £2.50 a day and normally they'd charge £8 per day. But even so initially, financially, it was terrible.

I had to give up my job because I basically couldn't do the hours. I'm a sales engineer and my bosses could, at the drop of a hat, want me to work until ten o'clock at night, Saturdays and Sundays, and I just couldn't do it. Things had to change.

I started looking for work and I'm really blessed because I've got a job that pays reasonably well and has given me a guaranteed commission for the first year. But I now have to pay a childminder. I drop Cassy off at the childminder at eight o'clock in the morning and pick her up at six. The childminder takes her to school and collects her at the end of every day. Now I feel I'm in a much better situation.

Practicalities

Let's look at some of the practical issues involved in stretching our time and money.

If your outgoings are greater than your income, you will need to tighten your belt. There's no getting away from it and it's better to do something now, rather than storing up bigger problems for yourself further down the line. If your children are old enough, sit down with them and explain the situation – ask them what you can do as a family to reduce your outgoings. It's important to limit your children's stress but it's also good for them to have some involvement and responsibility. It also gives you a base to go back to when they're demanding extras. You can remind them of the conversation you've had with them about money – and remind them that you're not being just a mean old miser.

My friend Evadne talked to her seventeen- and fifteen-year-old teenagers about finances. She felt dreadful doing it and felt as if she was losing her dignity – but it was worth it. She explained how they were limited financially – despite the fact that her ex-partner is very rich. The comparison between the situations of the two parents was dramatic and it was important that her girls understood. Evadne's children were old enough to have a clear grasp of the situation and afterwards she said there was a much greater honesty about how they all lived. By sharing and being honest the air was cleared between them all and, although their situation was still tough, they were able to plan ahead much more realistically.

Grace came from a very privileged background and for the last four years has battled in court because she felt it unfair that she should 'lower' herself financially when her husband left her. She's now at the point where she has to accept the situation she is in. The 'fighting' over money has put too much strain on her children. Grace says:

> *The sooner you explain the situation to your children, in a sensitive but clear manner, the better. Money is short when you get divorced – which is very sad, but that's just the way it is. I think it's important to make your children face the reality of divorce and move on rather than dragging out the pain or pretending it's going to be OK.*

Take a long look at how you spend money

Some people find it useful to have all direct debits and bills going out on a certain date in the month. If you can arrange for your income/benefit to come in before the essential bills go out then you will be able to see at a glance what you have for the rest of the month. It's helpful to know what you have available to spend.

Try not to fall into the trap that Denise found herself in. She's always struggled to make ends meet. So when she unexpectedly came into some money, instead of working out what bills needed paying, she understandably spent the lot on a luxurious American holiday as a treat for herself and her children. However, she immediately hit a wall of depression when she returned to a pile of red reminders, and memories of a great holiday faded instantly.

It can be frightening to face your real financial situation but the more you know the more control you have.

• Write down everything you spend money on for a month –

that means everything! This will be a real eye-opener in showing you where the money goes.

- Take a broader view of your whole year's expenses – when electricity/gas/insurance/phone bills come in – and work out the best way to pay them.
- If you need help working out a budget, ask a friend to help you. Get someone you trust to be on your case.
- See if there are any obvious areas where it would be easy for you to make savings.
- Once you know what you have to spend, work out a realistic budget.
- If at all possible have a small budget for the unexpected. If you have even a tiny amount in reserve for unforeseen expenses, you will feel more in control of your money.
- Allow a small amount of money for 'treats' – even if the treats are nothing more than a chocolate bar and a takeaway. It's important to build in things to look forward to when you're on a tight budget or you might end up abandoning the whole idea of controlling your money.
- Review your finances on a regular basis. The cost of living goes up; you might have a pay rise and so a new budget needs to be worked out. Personally I hate doing this but I force myself to review my finances every six months or so. When I can't face it I get my best friend to bully me into it!
- Once you've organised a budget, stick to it as best you can. Of course, unexpected expenditure will always catch you by surprise, but don't let it get you down. You may even find the very act of putting a budget together helps you minimise the number of unforeseen demands on your money.

Tip for success
If you have greater expenditure than income you should actually start addressing it now rather than a year down the road.

Facing the facts

Face your financial state as soon as possible. Chances are that the longer you leave it the worse it will become and you may end up with a serious debt and all the added stress that goes with it. Even though it's horrible to face now, the problem won't disappear and the longer you bury your head in the sand the worse the problem will eventually become. If your children are old enough it's a good idea to include them in the decisions about cutting corners.

I have a good friend whose financial situation took a radical nosedive. Some very difficult choices had to be made, which potentially included the family losing their home. She sat down with her girls and carefully explained the options. She said,

> *I need to know how you feel about all of this. I might not be able to do what you want but it is important for me to know how you feel so I can put it into the equation too.*

My friend was careful not to overburden her children by laying the final decision on them. The outcome was very positive. The girls said that being able to know the truth and air their views helped them feel 'listened to', 'included', and in a way they were able to accept the consequences of the final decision more easily.

Money-saving ideas

There are some practical steps we can take, which may help our situations . . .

1. If you buy a major item on credit, make sure that you fully understand the repayments and the deal you're getting. Don't be embarrassed to ask questions – make sure you can meet the payments before you sign on the dotted line. Check out how much you will actually pay if you buy on credit – you shouldn't have to pay three times the amount just because you want to pay in instalments. Look for cheaper ways to finance things. Talk to your bank manager!

2. Keep an eye open for 'interest free' sale times. Waiting a couple more months might mean you save several hundred pounds.

3. Even though it may be hard at the moment, try to take a long-term view. Think about pensions, savings and future security. You may not be able to save anything at the moment but have those ideas in mind for the future. Plan ahead wherever you can. It's worth mentioning that rules and regulations regarding financial rights and divorce are constantly changing. Your legal right to your partner's pension may change too – so be aware of how these changes may affect you.

4. You may receive offers in the post with a free fantastic gift – you sign for it; then, before you've realised it, you're up to your neck in interest – don't fall for it!

5. It's tempting to feel that having lots of store cards means greater status. I used to be very impressed by people who displayed loads of cards when they opened their wallets – now I worry for them. We're all often under the impression that we need a credit card for so many things (especially if we're buying via the telephone, by mail order or on the Internet) but you can use a debit card just as effectively.

6. Leave all credit/debit cards and chequebooks at home and use cash instead – it makes you far more careful about spending. There's nothing like seeing your hard-earned money part company with you to make you want to hang onto it! I tried it for a while and I made Scrooge look generous! I'm just about to embark on 'cash only' again as my spending needs rechecking – it's a good exercise for all of us. I know of one woman who has gone a step

further by freezing her credit card in a block of ice in the freezer at home. If she sees a 'must-have' purchase, she goes home and gets the ice block out. She then has about four hours to wait until the ice thaws (or an hour if she runs it under the hot tap!), during which time she thinks about whether she really can afford the item or not. You'll be unsurprised to learn that, by the time the credit card has thawed out, she's normally decided to save her money!

7. Beware of cold callers, whether on doorstep or telephone. Some salespeople will hard sell to get you to buy things you don't want and can't afford to push up their commission. Telling them that you have no money might not put some of them off! If you have signed up for something you don't want, take advantage of the cooling-off period many reputable firms offer – within that period you can change your mind.

8. Remember that the packaging can make things look very attractive – it's meant to sell the product so don't be seduced into buying stuff you don't need!!

9. Find an efficient and practical way to do your weekly food shop, one that works for you. I know one friend who will never go shopping without a list; it cuts down impulse-buying that can throw the budget. Try to establish an agreement with your children as to when they can have sweets. It won't necessarily remove constant requests of 'Can I have?' but it gives a better framework in which to deal with them. For those of us who are lucky enough to have computers and are on-line, there may be some mileage in having our shopping delivered. The minimal charge may well be balanced by the reduced temptation to spend and the time we gain in return.

10. Don't be afraid to ask for help. There are a variety of organisations (such as Gingerbread and Credit Action)

that can give you advice – details are in the back of this book.

> ### Tip for success
> Remember that it's never been easier to spend money that we don't have.

Getting a grip

Getting a grip on finances can be hard and, though cold comfort, it is not unique to those of us who are single parents. One woman told her husband that they spent £300 more per month than they earned and his reaction was to say, 'I refuse to believe that!' That's a common reaction.

THE FIRST STEP IN DEALING WITH DEBT IS FACING UP TO IT...

THANKS— THAT ADVICE IS PRICELESS.

Ellie was given a book because she had so many debts and needed help. The book went through the things we're all taught about money and our attitudes towards spending and saving. Ellie found it hugely helpful. She'd been on income support for several months and received no maintenance from her ex-husband. She worked out that she was an image-spender and wanted to spend to keep up with the right group – which meant having the right clothes and everything else that goes with it. She also wanted to be generous and would often end up paying for the group when she was out. Realising that's the sort of person she was helped her to control her spending. Now she's sorted out her finance and she managed to do it while on benefit!

Keeping a balance

You may feel that you are in the most unsolvable situation – especially if you live in a metropolitan centre where mortgages and rents are high and the cost of living is astronomical.

I can't begin to pretend to have all the answers, but sometimes there are practical solutions to some of our problems. For example, I have a friend whose daughter is a real fashion 'victim' and until recently wasn't interested in anything other than clothes shopping. (This is, as you can imagine, an expensive pastime and one which will cause tension between a parent and child when finances are already stretched.) However, one weekend, much against the daughter's will, her mother abandoned the regular shopping ritual for a day out walking in the country – in the rain! After an initial (expected) reluctance, her daughter discovered that splashing her mother in puddles and climbing trees was exhilarating. She revelled in getting dirty and mucky and positively glowed from this new-found freedom. They now spend most weekends 'actively' out of town!

My niece recently told me that one of the things she loves doing most is playing 'Pass the Pigs'! For her, an evening playing board-games with her mum and brothers is preferable to almost anything else. It costs nothing, especially as the game came as a Christmas present, but best of all it gives her mum the chance to show her children how valued they are, just by spending time with them!

There are places to take your children that won't cost you anything at all – you might be surprised how much is around. Turn it into a challenge – it doesn't have to cost the earth to be fun! Particularly if you have younger children, find out if there are toy libraries near you as well as ordinary libraries. Search out the sort of items you can borrow rather than buy. Read your local paper to find out if there is something you can take your child to for free. You might be surprised by what's around – especially during school holidays.

Hazel has three grown-up children. Money was scarce when the children were little and Hazel had to find inexpensive ways of amusing her kids. For Hazel, though, the great times she had with her children outweighed the financial struggle:

I am now forty-eight and look back on the time I stayed at home bringing up my three children (now twenty-three, twenty-one and nineteen) as the most rewarding time of my life. I never considered staying at work after the birth of my first child. I did not want anyone else to be the first one to see a tooth, a smile, a first step. I wanted to be the one who influenced their learning and development.

Being a mother involves a great deal of giving, but this is counteracted by the joy children give in return. Children reveal the wonder of things we consider 'everyday' – the sheer pleasure of curling up in a chair with one (or all!) of them on your lap and venturing into the pages of a book; watching them learn as they play; noting their different personalities and how they respond in their own ways to the world.

It's not all a bed of roses. Babies can cry through the night (often for no apparent reason) and you can be so tired you don't know what day it is. But if you're home, you can grab a nap when they do. You sit with them when they are sick, but your presence brings great comfort. They can be demanding and noisy, but trying to understand what drives them makes life interesting.

Instead of having a few hours with them, you spend your life with them – you are their security, the rock from which they venture forth, and you are still there when they need to come back. Now, my children say how important it was that their 'rock' was always there to hear about their troubles and successes. Life wasn't wholly for the children, however. I managed to see my friends and play sport every week.

We were not well off. The reality was that we qualified for free milk and social support. We sold the car and had no holiday for several years, but we were very happy. Children like to be where you are. You can take them for walks and to the park. You can read to them, play with them, set them up Wendy houses under the table, cook with them. You see other friends and chat to them while your children play, so all your talk need not be just to children.

No money could buy the joys of that time and I wouldn't have wanted to pay someone else to do all these things. It wasn't for long. I have sat on hillsides watching birds, chased round stations taking train numbers, watched umpteen ballet rehearsals, sewn numerous costumes and darned ballet shoes. I have been teacher, nurse, psychiatrist, storyteller, counsellor, yes, and head cook and bottle-washer, cleaner and laundry woman – many roles, and because I was at home, I had the time to do these things, not just a hurried couple of hours after work when I would have been exhausted.

I work full time now, but giving time up to my children

IS YOUR FAMILY RICH?

MUST BE – MUM ALWAYS SAYS SHE TREASURES ME.

when they were small doesn't mean my personality died! I am back studying at school, I go to the theatre and the ballet, we go abroad for holidays, and I have become skilled in many aspects of computing. Best of all, though, I have a wonderful relationship with my children. We went on a canal-boat holiday last year and they chose to come with us. They don't need me in the same way now, but the deep relationship that forms when you share lives is strong and binding. For me, the very best word to hear in the whole world is 'Mum'!

A time for everything

However hard life may be for you at the moment, it's worth saying that periods of grave financial difficulty don't usually go on forever. At least in relative terms, some times are better than others. The key is to accept where you are at the moment, take some control – it may mean some tough decisions – and realise that you *can* go forward. We need to be good stewards of our money and wise in our spending without forgetting that giving is good – whatever your circumstances. We live in a world dominated by lack of time and, as single parents, our time can often feel as precious as our finances but remember that there are many small opportunities to give. We feel good when we give something to someone else, whether it's time or money, and it's a good habit to pass on to our children.

Tip for success
Small acts of generosity can make a big difference.

Will you?

One aspect that is often overlooked is that of wills. We are so busy with the present that we give little thought to the future, even though writing a will can be done quickly and easily. As I know only too well, the unexpected does happen from time to time and all parents want to know that their children will be well taken care of. Not all families are as supportive as mine has been. Wills aren't just about money, about the 'who gets what' – they're also about who takes care of our children if we die unexpectedly. Solicitors will draw up wills for a fee, but it's down to you to formally ask friends or family to become guardians of your children. For some single parents who don't have supportive families it can be a real worry – not knowing where the children would go if the worst happened. Talk to close, trusted friends and find those who would be willing to be named as guardians of your children in your will – and who your children would be happy living with. By sorting it out legally now, you can put your mind at rest and make the prospect of a difficult situation a little easier for your children.

Seeing light at the end of the tunnel

As single parents, the challenge of constantly juggling and tightrope walking can be exhausting. At times it may seem that the choices open to us are so limited that it feels like no choice at all. However, it is possible to choose how we view whatever situation we find ourselves in.

The Austrian psychologist Viktor Frankl, who overcame the horrors of a Nazi concentration camp, was obviously intrigued at what it was that enabled him and other survivors to endure conditions that caused death to many. After much investigation he discovered that those who survived the concentration camp horrors all had one thing in common – they had a vision for the future and a sense that they still had some important work to do. Vision is the key to survival, and much research supports this view.

So it seems to me that no matter how difficult things are or can be we have to remain hopeful. First, nobody's life stands still – we are on a journey. Even if we find ourselves in the worst work/family dilemma, it doesn't mean it has to stay this way. Second, we can take encouragement from Viktor Frankl because even amid the most unimaginable cruelty he, and others, didn't give up; they dreamed their dreams. And it was their daydreaming that kept them alive. We too can be encouraged and motivated by our future-oriented visions.

Tip for success
Nobody's life stands still. So, whatever your situation, have hope for the future.

Choice

There is no doubt that for single parents the question of finance and the issues and decisions surrounding it are complex and sometimes *very* stressful. But with effort we *can* be proactive; we *can* choose and make choices based on our values and principles, not just our circumstances. We *can* focus on what we believe is our goal and walk our carefully balanced tightrope towards it. We *can* juggle our lives around our priorities, our vision, our values. We *can* find a way that is beneficial to us all – our children, our employers and ourselves – by constantly reviewing and reassessing our situation, enabling us to be *more effective parents*.

8
Where Do We Go from Here?

Keeping Healthy Relationships

Our unique situation means that Justine and I haven't had to face the wrangling, negotiation and accountability that arise from dealing with an estranged partner. However, due to my sister's death I do know what it is to have the responsibility of explaining complex and devastating changes in a way that a child can digest.

I now realise that most of the basic principles needed to deal with an estranged partner are actually fundamental to success in all relationships. The issue of maintaining healthy relationships is relevant to us all.

What if ...

Not all relationships break down because someone walks out. It may be that you are a single parent because your partner has died either suddenly and unexpectedly or after a long illness. The initial reaction in these situations will be shock, especially if your partner died in an accident or even committed suicide. There are no straightforward, easy answers as to how to deal with your child in this situation. You will have your own emotions to cope with as well as those of your child. The way in which you talk to your child about her parent will need to be sensitive and careful but, from my own and others' experience, honesty is always the best policy. There are many questions to which we don't know the answers. Inventing complex stories in order to make our children feel better is ultimately only likely to lead to trouble further down the road and may well cause more hurt than the truth.

You will have your own feelings of abandonment to deal with as well as those of your child. If your partner has died you need to allow yourself and your child a lot of space. Grieving is a long process, which sometimes takes years to work through. You may get support from friends and relatives at the beginning, but before very long life will settle into some kind of pattern and people will think that you're OK. Perhaps only a few people who are really close to you will know that you are still struggling to come to terms with your loss. Never be afraid to shout for help and say that you're not coping. If you feel that you have nobody to turn to, contact a bereavement counselling service – find someone at the end of a phone to talk to. Sometimes it's easier to talk to strangers than close friends who will be coping with their own grief over the same loss.

During the grieving process, both you and your child are likely to experience feelings of hurt and anger, shock, loss and sadness. Your child may express those feelings in different ways and may feel them at different moments to you so, although you'll both be grieving together, you may reach different stages at different times. Your child may not express her feelings the same way as you, so be aware you'll need to allow her to deal with her feelings in her own way. How your child copes will depend very much on how old she is and the sort of person she is. Whatever her personality, however, she will need a lot of reassurance – she will want to know that you aren't going to suddenly disappear as well.

Talk to your child – at the level at which she can understand – about the person you've both lost. You'll be able to share good memories and remember things that made you laugh together. You'll be able to celebrate their life. Keep any mementoes, however small, for the future. You and your child will be able to look at and talk about these things as your child grows up. Your child will need some tangible reminders of her mum or dad as she learns to deal with the loss. If your child is still a baby, you will be able to have such conversations – but when she's older. Then it will be for you to tell your child about the good things she shared with her mum or dad when she was tiny and how much her parent loved her.

Tip for success
Whatever your feelings, give your children permission, room and time to grieve. They will have lost part of themselves too.

Thermometers

Children are the most amazing thermometers! At every age they can, it seems, assess the temperature of our moods with alarming accuracy. A child's perception that 'something is wrong' is quite often far more accurate than that which most adults around us could make. In many cases, their own emotions and anxieties may become entangled with ours.

Maintaining healthy relationships, wherever possible, will help to reduce the stress all round and, in particular of course, when dealing with 'the ex'. Our success is measured by keeping our past relationships on an even keel. This will have a very positive effect on our children.

Regardless of the quality of relationship with your former partner, you will now have the responsibility of bringing up your child jointly, but separately. In whatever you do try to take a consistent approach, avoiding two completely different parenting styles being thrown at one child. If your relationship is amicable:

• Sit down together and work through key issues.

- Lay down some guidelines, if at all possible, on how you will be consistent.
- Try to agree on bedtimes, pocket money, sweets, homework – even girl/boyfriends! It will help reduce the incidences of 'But Mummy always lets me stay up late'.
- Don't be tempted to buy favour with your child.
- Stick to the arrangements you have made.

Keep the lines of communication open between you and work hard to avoid relegating your child to the role of 'go-between'. On the one hand, it's not fair for your child, and neither is it a recipe for success in 'separate' parenting. As well as being thermometers, children are expert wooden spoons and can stir a situation beautifully – playing each parent off the other! If, on the other hand, your relationship with your former partner is less than amicable, still do everything *you* can to keep the lines of communication open.

Tip for success
Remember, children need a consistent approach
from both parents.

I'm feeling a little tense, dear

Children are very good at picking up vibes from their parents. They're very sensitive to our moods – even young toddlers. If we can explain to our children why we're feeling anxious it will help them to understand and they may not be so worried by our behaviour. It will give them something to focus on – 'Oh, Dad's grumpy because the phone bill came in' is much easier for a child to handle than non-specific tears and tantrums. In the face of no obvious explanation for Mum or Dad's bad mood, some children will assume they're at fault, so be sure that your children know that *they* are not the problem.

Estranged families

You may no longer live with your ex, but they are still the parent of your children. They will still be part of your child's life, in a very real way, even if they are absent. In fact whether or not we care to admit it, without them our beautiful children wouldn't exist. Dismissing the ex in front of your child may be interpreted as a dismissal of them too – so be careful not to do it. It's important that your child never feels that the break-up was anything to do with them. Of course, it's also quite likely that our children will miss their estranged mum or dad. Whether we like it or not, they're still your child's mum or dad and, as a result, a big part of your child's life, so one of the most harmful things we can do to our children is to alienate them from that parent.

If your partner has left you – for whatever reason – you might feel hard done by. After all, you are the one who has to pick up the pieces of both your own life and your child's – and that is no easy task. You will suddenly find that you are the breadwinner and the one who looks after your child. All the decisions that have to be made now fall squarely on your shoulders and you're the one running around frantically making phone calls to sort out childcare at 7.30 a.m. on a Monday morning after the childminder has called in sick. It's not surprising that your feelings towards your ex are less than warm.

All by myself

In addition to your own feelings you have to cope with your child's. It's easy to underestimate the complex tensions that accompany divorce – even a fairly amicable one. Your child may be angry and upset because one of her parents has left, but as you're the only parent around for her to vent her feelings on she's likely to take it out on you. Your child may become sullen and awkward or loud and angry. It's very hard for you on top of everything else that you have to cope with. However, try not to take it personally – try to understand your child's feeling of dislocation and take a positive view. If you allow your child to express herself, however negative the emotion, it will do you both good. She won't be bottling it up and festering bad feelings towards both of you. The old saying is true that we hurt the ones we love and who we are closest to.

Whatever happens, don't worry about justifying your position:

- If your child starts lobbing all kinds of false accusations at you in the heat of the moment, don't argue back. Leave it until she's calmed down and is in a more receptive mood to talk more rationally.
- When she's calm you'll be able to talk through her feelings

at a level at which she can understand, depending on how old she is.

- Don't give her more information than she's asking for but instead try tackling how both of you are feeling.
- You'll need to avoid the pitfall of 'slagging off' your ex-partner, however tempting it is. You may think that by doing that you'll cement the bond between you and your child but it can be damaging to your relationship in the long term. Somewhere down the line your child may construe your comments as your attempt to turn her against the parent who left. Instead, be willing to talk about your ex with your children and speak positively when you do. Avoid trying to look good at your ex-partner's expense. After all, though it might not always seem like it, it really isn't a competition.
- Be honest – but be as positive about the situation as you can.

Jackie's husband left when her son was five – and her son responded by being angry with her. She says, 'I'll never forget the time when he looked up at me, a five-year-old face, full of fury. I thought that's not fair – I tried so much – I went through counselling. And now my child is mad at me!'

It may be a bitter pill to swallow but whatever circumstances led to the breakdown of your relationship, forgiveness is almost certainly the key to move forward.

Tip for success
Forgiveness is the key to moving on.

Oh, you know it ain't easy

Melissa, a single mum whose partner left her and their children, has found forgiveness to be crucial in dealing with the pain:

I thought I'd forgiven everyone in the entire world but whenever I sit down and think about it something else comes up that I've not even thought of. There are layers of forgiveness. You may even need to forgive yourself – which can be hard to do. It's wonderful to clear out your mind, clear out your heart and make room for wholesome things to come in. Then it's important to sit down with the child and talk about the pain so that they can deal with it too.

It's worth noting here that forgiving your ex-partner doesn't mean that life will suddenly become a bed of roses when it comes to your relationship with them. Forgiveness will free you, however, and it may well improve your relationship with your ex into the bargain. At the end of the day, it might not make any difference to your ex's behaviour so you may well have to keep forgiving.

- It takes effort to forgive.
- You may have to forgive your ex-partner many times.
- You may have to forgive yourself.
- Teach your child how to be forgiving.
- Forgiveness helps you all to move on.

Tip for success
Even when you're tired of it, never stop doing the right thing.

Maintaining civility

However bitter you may feel towards your ex, however hard you may find it to forgive, maintaining a degree of civility with them is crucial to maintaining an overall status quo.

Remember: The only person you have complete control over is yourself.

You will not be able to control what your ex-partner does or says but you can control your own actions. No matter how much you *encourage* someone else to do the right thing, you can never *make* them. For example, you might rightly believe that your children shouldn't be the battleground between you and your partner. However, if your partner continues to use them as pawns, your best move is to refuse to play chess!

The greatest temptation, particularly if your partner is behaving obnoxiously, is to return like with like, but such acrimony can detrimentally affect your child even more than the break-up itself.

I know I sound idealistic, but I believe we must at least strive for ideals. However, I'm also aware that there are some situations where civility is *truly* impossible and for such cases you may be well advised to contact organisations such as the National Association of Child Contact Centres. These organisations can go some way in offering small practical solutions to large and complex problems. For example, providing a 'neutral territory' to drop off and pick up a child visiting the other parent.

Miracles still happen

My friend Jackie talked to me about having to be gracious towards her ex-husband. There were times when he did things that made her furious. But instead of shouting at him she'd bite her tongue and try to be gracious. At first she was gracious through gritted teeth but she likened it to getting on an exercise bike and saying, 'OK, I'm going to do two minutes today, but at least I've started – tomorrow I'll stay on for four minutes.' Now, after a long period of 'training', she really has forgiven him and their relationship is far healthier. Even she can't believe her change of heart!

Guidelines

Children find divorce and family break-up just as hard – if not harder – than adults. It can be a lonely and confusing place for them. Here are some basic guidelines to help you get your child through this difficult time. They have been drawn from the experience of mums and dads who have had broken relationships and largely assume there will be a desire on the part of the other parent to see the child, although I know this is not always the case.

1. If at all possible, be positive about your ex-partner. At the very least try not to be negative. Tell your child that both of you love her.
2. Don't criticise your ex to your children – keep in mind that it's their mum or dad you are talking about. Whatever may have happened between the two of you, your child will have some loyalty to both. Even if the other parent criticises you, try not to retaliate.

WHAT ARE DAD'S GOOD POINTS?

ER... BEING YOUR DAD?

3. Leave photos of the missing parent around, use their name – it helps your child. It's important that your ex is still part of your child's life. You don't have to offer up

discussion if your child isn't asking – but be ready to talk. Give your child permission to talk about the other parent; give your child permission to miss the other parent. It will help her come to terms with her new situation.

4. Encourage your child to keep in contact with her non-resident parent. She could send text messages or e-mails as well as use the more traditional phone call or letter. Make a point of ensuring that you remind her to send birthday cards, etc.

5. Try to encourage your child to see her mum or dad – even though that could be unbelievably difficult if the parent shows no interest. By encouraging the relationship, however, you are at least keeping the doors open for better things to come. It's good for your child to see that you are not blocking the relationship.

6. Don't use your child as a messenger or a spy. Children shouldn't be drawn into adult games or used as pawns. Keep *your* relationship with your ex separate from your children's.

7. Discuss with your ex about Christmas, weekends, and who is going to have who and when. And then stick to the arrangements as much as possible. Write things down on a calendar or in a diary. Even if your ex doesn't stick to their plans try to stick to yours – it brings stability into the situation.

8. Encourage your child to continue their relationship with the other parent. There will be long-term issues to work out and face and the quicker you do that the easier it will be.

9. It's important that you keep your promises to your child. She may feel let down by one or both of her parents so only make promises to her that you can keep.

10. Keep on reassuring your child that the break-up is nothing to do with her – especially if your child continues to seem anxious about it. It's important that your child doesn't blame herself.

If your child is young, it may be helpful to keep all correspondence from the other parent – things such as birthday cards, letters, etc. They might be useful later on, once your child is old enough to discuss things with you in more depth.

Tip for success

Remember that children find separation just as hard as – if not harder than – adults do.

Now you see me...

Another of the hardest situations to handle with your children must be when your former partner doesn't want contact with them. Simpler, perhaps, for your sanity, but a nightmare in how you handle the situation with regards to your children. How do you explain someone disappearing out of their world? Where to begin?

One of the difficult areas to deal with is the knowledge that your partner could walk back into the life of both you and your child at any time – even if they don't. You may well feel as if you're in a state of limbo – unable to move on – to begin with, as you'll always be looking over your shoulder or waiting for a ring on the doorbell in case your partner has had a change of heart. That possibility always exists. Your child may be hoping that her mum or dad will suddenly get in contact. Children like to believe in happy endings – that it will all work out right in the end.

As reality begins to dawn that, perhaps, Daddy or Mummy just isn't coming back, your child may experience an overwhelming sense of rejection – and could easily start blaming herself. Offer lots of reassurance. Sometimes there are no simple explanations for why a parent doesn't want to see their child any more. Again, honesty is the best policy. Don't tell your child a lie to try to protect her – it will only cause trouble in the long run. Try to be as open as you can without overloading your child with information or your own bad feelings. The best thing that you can do is to rebuild your life and to move on.

Sophie's partner walked out without any warning, leaving her to deal with their children. She tried to protect them from the pain of truth but found this made a difficult situation worse:

> *I had to see a child psychiatrist because my husband had disappeared without a trace from my children's lives and mine. One minute my children had a father and the next minute he was completely gone. I tried to protect them from their pain, because I thought if they knew what happened to their dad it would hurt them even more, so his name was not mentioned in the house. The problem was that the children bottled it up and their unhappiness manifested itself in antisocial behaviour and bed-wetting.*

Let me tell you a story

One good way of talking through these things is to get one of the many excellent children's books on the subject. If it's hard for your child to talk to you, you might find your child will open up when you're reading together. Ask at your local library for any good children's books that deal with divorce and separation. Puppets are another useful means of opening up communication for young children. You can act out little plays with hand puppets or dolls and toy characters (not quite as effective if they're sixteen-plus!) and through the actions and conversations you can express what's been going on. Take this at your child's pace – and gently. It's amazing what a child will tell a puppet that she wouldn't dream of telling you in any other way. So look out for these opportunities to act out stories. Your child will know what you're doing and you'll know what you're doing, but it's non-threatening.

It may also be that your child would benefit from professional counselling. *This is perfectly fine!* Even today counselling is still largely considered a taboo area, often associated with failure. Sometimes, it's easier to cope with the effects of our children's pain than admit they have a problem, which we may have contributed to and for which they now need help. Don't allow your pride to prevent you from doing what you know is best. No family breakdown is ever 'pain free' for you *or* your child. Sometimes it will be difficult to assess your child's emotional state on the surface. From toddlers to teenagers, though, emotional turmoil has a way of manifesting itself in a variety of ways, not all as obvious as others.

Counselling for children and young people can be amazingly positive and beneficial. If you are aware that your child is experiencing particular difficulties you should contact your GP. Your GP will want to check to make sure there are no underlying medical causes for any changes in your child's behaviour, before pointing you in the right direction for professional counselling.

Tip for success
Be courageous: Acknowledge problems and deal with them.

In-laws or outlaws?

The breakdown of a relationship, which results in the absence of a partner, is painful enough but few are prepared for the complex scenarios which can evolve concerning the 'in-laws'. This could well be another situation that calls for your sacrificial love. It's a situation where you may have to do the right thing for your child even if it's not what you would want to happen. Seeing and being in contact with in-laws may be an unpleasant or painful experience for you – especially if they have clearly taken sides with their own child – but they are still a very relevant part of your child's family, their culture, their heritage. Where possible you should encourage contact, not deny it.

This is also true in circumstances where a parent has been

bereaved. It's easy to slip into a life of your own which doesn't include your in-laws – you may have never been close to them – but if your partner has died it's really important for your child to feel connected to her mum or dad's side of the family. After all, children have an inherent need to know where they have come from *and* who they are part of.

> **Tip for success**
> Encourage your child's sense of family to include *all* relatives.

Simon, a single dad, whose in-laws are both frail, says, 'I really encourage my son to have a good relationship with my in-laws because he is a real light to them. He brings a real sense of joy into their lives, and they reciprocate this to him.'

Healthy relationships – including those with the ex – need to be worked at. Their success doesn't occur overnight and often calls for much personal sacrifice, but it's worth all our effort in order to provide as stable an environment for our children as possible.

9
New Beginnings
Adapting to a new family shape

My daughter Justine's best friend Rachel happens to be the daughter of my best friend Sue! As a consequence both homes (despite the twenty miles' distance between them) are virtually interchangeable. There are of course many benefits to this arrangement. Justine and I have a 'home' in the country and they have a 'pad' in town. Justine no longer has the disappointment of (at best) terribly bland food, as Sue is a brilliant cook; and Rachel no longer suffers the humiliation of poorly darned clothes, as I am an impressive seamstress. Justine and I also get on brilliantly with Mike, Sue's husband, who incidentally (despite seriously bad jokes) is a wonderful 'Mr Fix-It'. Samantha, Rachel's younger sister, is not only totally adored by Justine and me but over the last few years seems to have inherited a laugh uncannily similar to mine . . .

Add to this, 'extended-family' holidays, happy birthdays, joyful Easters and Christmases crammed around either my or Sue's dining-tables (!) and the result is an eccentric but very satisfactory arrangement built on mutual love, respect and security.

I have learned that families exist in all shapes and sizes, for a variety of reasons. I've also learned that at the heart of any healthy, well-balanced family is relationship. There's a well-known adage that says you can judge a man by the company he keeps. Whether we agree with that or not, most of us *would* agree that our close relationships, both platonic and non-platonic, have an effect on us and to an extent influence our character and values and therefore, by default, affect our children.

It's crucial that through observing my relationships, my daughter learns the value and the stability of good friendships. I hope Justine realises that relationships – all relationships – need to be tended and nurtured in order to succeed. I hope she will realise that taking time to build strong and lasting relationships can be the soundest investment she will ever make. I hope she will learn that, unlike so many things in our society, relationships aren't to be 'thrown away'. I hope she understands that friendship is a commitment.

It's a lot easier to address these issues within our platonic friendships. After all, they are rarely perceived as a threat by our children. But what about friendships that might lead to a binding change in our family shape?

Party time!

There's no doubt that a great deal of thought and consideration needs to go into a new relationship. There's no getting away from the fact that it's much harder to start a new relationship when you have children – after all, it's not just you that you have to think about. You're automatically restricted by your responsibilities – it's not so easy to be the life and soul of the party when you are permanently exhausted and finding it difficult to get a childminder. The question 'How do I meet someone new?' may not even be top of your list of priorities.

Wendy, a single mum, says:

> *I would not want a new boyfriend unless I was going to have a long-term relationship with him – because I just don't want to open a can of worms that I cannot close. And the fact is we're very vulnerable . . . I don't think married people know how difficult it is.*

You may feel that your children need so much of your time that you don't have the energy to start a new relationship. Some think that really you should wait until your children grow up before you remarry or begin a permanent relationship – it is so much easier, especially when the children have been through the trauma of a divorce. Having to accept someone else into their life who will start to give them rules and regulations can be difficult – the problem is they can't just jump into Mummy or Daddy's bed, there's someone else in there now! However,

- Remember that you don't have to put your life on hold because you have children.
- Find time to go out – even if it's only once in a while and you have to book it up a long way in advance.
- Make the effort to go out for the occasional evening – sometimes it's easier to just stay in and have an early night, but a night out will do you good.
- Don't be afraid to start up conversations with people you'd like to get to know better. You may be out of practice, but there's no better way to get back into it!
- Remember that new relationships can begin at any time and in any place; sometimes they happen when you're least expecting them! That said, avoid the hunt for a new partner becoming an all-consuming task!
- When you do strike up a new friendship it's important that you're honest from the outset about your children. You don't want to lead anyone up the garden path!

Tip for success
Make the effort to go out – even if it's only very occasionally.

Buses

Remember how, as a teenager, there was never anyone around when you were desperate to have a boy/girlfriend? And then, when you relaxed about it, like buses, three turned up at once? People sense when you are needy and may give you a wide berth, but when you're more relaxed and comfortable with yourself it is a different story. It's a good idea to get rid of as much emotional baggage as possible, before you embark on a new relationship. I am aware that this is easier said than done but, at the risk of repeating myself, it really is vital that we get our priorities right. We need to accept responsibility for our own emotional wellbeing and our own behaviour and be proactive within our own lives. Ultimately this will mean that all our relationships will be more healthy and fulfilling.

Eyes wide open

A new relationship will have its ups and downs, however much better it may be than the old one, or than being on our own. Relationships have to be worked at – and hiccups along the way are not necessarily a sign that the world is going to come crashing round your ears or your particular knight or damsel is about to run off into the distance alone!

If you think you're ready for another relationship, ask yourself these questions:

- Am I coping and content with my life at the moment?
- Am I living in the present or the past?
- Have I learned to be alone without experiencing loneliness?
- Can I be content on my own?
- Do I know my weaknesses?
- Do I want companionship or a long-term relationship?

And later on in the relationship you might need to ask yourself:

- At what point does someone become part of the family?
- At what point will I allow someone to make decisions with me that may affect the whole family?

Everyone will answer differently and there are no rules to follow in this game. It's common sense, but try not to jump into another relationship just because you can't cope with being alone. Be honest with yourself! It may well be that, after all, you simply want companionship rather than a long-term commitment. It's important that you know what you want from a relationship before you start. There's no benefit to be had by jumping out of the frying-pan into the fire – out of loneliness and into a disastrous relationship. Once you *do* feel ready to start another relationship, whether you're looking for a new partner or for someone who is simply a good friend, the same advice applies – despite the temptation, there's no need to rush!

Tip for success
There's no need to rush into another relationship
– take your time!

If someone else does come along, try to enter that relationship with your eyes wide open. We are too easily seduced by the romantic myth of love – the old ideal that there is one perfect person in the world for us. It's understandable – after all, we all want to be loved and cared for. Some people spend their lives looking for that person – only to be disappointed ten years down the line. Reality is very different. Falling in love is one thing – making a relationship work when the fuzzy feelings have worn off is something else altogether!

Riding off into the sunset?

Rita's husband left her and she was on her own for five years. Then she met Lewis who was a bachelor without children. They waited for five years and finally married. The problems they faced were very different from the problems that Rita faced with her first husband.

First of all they had huge financial problems and Rita's son did not get on with his stepfather. Then, three years into their marriage Lewis had a stroke even though he was only forty-two years old – for one whole summer he was half-paralysed. Lewis has still not made a full recovery.

Rita loves her husband enormously but has found remarriage difficult. It's easy to pin our hopes on the 'second time around' being the answer to all our problems. We might be tempted to believe that, although things didn't work out once, there's a knight (and knights needn't be male!) in shining armour waiting round the corner. It's vital that you don't assume that financial or any other problems will disappear just because you remarry. Try to take a cold calculated look at the situation you are going in to. Look at the practicalities and ask yourself if you truly believe you can make the situation work.

Tip for success
Avoid letting your desire for a boy/girlfriend relationship become an all-consuming passion; make the most of your life as it is now.

The pieces won't fit together

It may be that you have your child to stay with you only at weekends or in school holidays and this may bring about its own problems for you in terms of developing a new relationship. My friend James, who has his son every weekend, says that he often feels as if he's living a dual existence:

> *You may find that you live a disjointed life. There's the logistical issue of being a single parent one minute and a single person the next. So you will have to be particularly deft at organisation, at being with the right people at the right times – and letting them be aware that you're available to be included. Feeling sorry for yourself because of this disjointed existence is not the answer!*

We are all creatures of habit and some of us find it harder than others to make the transition between single person and single parent. If your child is with you only part of the time you may find yourself surprised to have her in the back seat of the car when you go shopping! You may feel as if you have a split personality; one minute you're a parent and the next you are a free agent. Inconsistencies cause stress so don't be surprised if that's how you're feeling.

Avoid dwelling on the negative aspects of your situation. Aim, instead, to have a diverse and full life and enjoy your children when they're with you. Make the most of their company. When you're on your own, you'll find it easier to go out and about and meet new people – there are a lot of things you will be able to do on your own that you couldn't do with a child – so make the most of these times too. Your happiness will rub off on your children when they're with you.

If you should meet a potential new partner, it's really important to be honest with them about your domestic circumstances from the very outset. They may think that you're footloose and fancy-free if your child is living with your ex-partner. It's always better to be clear, right from the beginning, as to where your responsibilities lie – it will avoid problems further down the line.

Steve, a single dad has also found sharing childcare with his ex-partner to be very disjointed:

> *When my son spends weekends with his mum I don't really spend much time on my own. I have loads of interests. I run a lot – I'm training right now for a marathon. I've got a boat, so I get out on the boat. And I like being out at lots of parties and things. I'm just in the throes of a lot of change now, and I'll probably end up moving to the country on a three-day-a-week basis – nearer to him. Even with spending three days there and four here, it's still a bit disjointed, isn't it?*

Stability

When we begin a new non-platonic relationship, however well intended, there's no guarantee that it will be a lifelong commitment. The time to stop and think is *before* making another commitment – a case of look before you leap rather than jump and hope for the best!

We have to begin by putting first things first. We have to be clear in our own minds what our values are and, perhaps more crucially, what our most important priorities are. Remembering that we are our children's role models, as well as their source of stability, it's imperative that we think about our relationships and how they affect our children. Our children are the permanent part of our lives – and we of theirs – and they need security. It can be very hard on a child if she has a whole string of 'aunties' and 'uncles' to cope with.

Responsibility

Sharon introduced a new partner into her family unit quite soon after meeting him. Even though he wasn't living with them, she had introduced a stranger into the family. At the same time, Sharon got a promotion at work and spent more time in the office than she needed, relying on her new partner to keep the family going. The two things combined together had a massive impact on the stability of Sharon's family. She suddenly realised that what had been a happy and stable unit had spiralled into chaos. Sharon decided that the only way out of the chaos was to work just the necessary hours at the office, which would give her a little extra time at home. Being at home more meant that Sharon was more in tune with the family dynamics. She had more time to consider the decisions that had to be made rather than leaving them for someone else to make – someone who wasn't so connected to her children. It took a little while, but eventually Sharon managed to get family life back onto an even keel.

When we have carried the weight of responsibility for our children it can seem a wonderful idea to hand over the burden to someone else. However tempting it may be, though, it's important that we don't hand over responsibility for our family to our new partner. In time, we may be able to share that responsibility but, in the meantime, we need to carry on making the decisions that are best for us and our children. After all, however much of a saint our new partner may be, we're still the ones who know our children best.

Tip for success
Try to keep stability in your family unit when you introduce a new partner.

Baggage

We all carry baggage with us and if we've had a painful, broken relationship we may have a *lot* to carry. Remember the best any parent can do is to sort out as much of that baggage as possible. Experience is something we can all learn from. Everybody has things in their life that they wish they hadn't done – or things they wish they *had* done. Regret is common to all parents, but we can use our past mistakes to inform the decisions we make now. Even bad experiences can be transformed into springboards if we learn from them to make the future better.

Be aware of the hurt that you carry and how you might react. Insecurity and jealousy are a potent mix that can do irreparable damage. Try not to let things get out of proportion. Trust takes time to build and both you and your new partner may have to work at it.

There is also the issue of building the relationship between a new boy/girlfriend and your child. Again, this may take time and its progress will vary greatly depending on the age and personalities of our children. Remember they too may bring their emotional scars with them, scars that may not have healed at the same rate as yours. This is why it is crucial for you to continually evaluate your situation and be honest about the impact it is having. Remember, y*ou* are still the one in control.

Hanni, a single dad, has found that there is an awful lot to think about when entering a new relationship. His priorities are very different now that he has a son to think about:

My son knows instinctively who are mates and who is something more. He has his own way of showing me that. He does little skits, he goes 'I'm in lurve' – he's really funny actually – but I think probably one difficulty is the older you get the more you realise the complexity of relationships.

As a single guy, a lot of the women I might be attracted to or who might be attracted to me have got kids and, because you know the damage that gets done when separation occurs, it makes you less likely to want to get involved. You become more discerning; you know exactly what you need and what you don't need. It's hard for someone else to come into your life, because you've actually got a family. And you have patterns that are pretty non-negotiable because your child has to come first – which is really hard when you go into a new relationship.

If somebody else is coming from another family and they're bringing their children, and you're still dealing with your ex, it becomes even more involved! There's your ex and you, your new partner and their ex, your children and their children and you're all trying to be parents . . . aargh!

The relationships between parents, their children and potential new partners and their children can be extremely complicated! Before we have children we only have to think about ourselves, but once we have children the whole picture changes. We look for different things in a partner. It becomes important for us to know if a new partner gets on well with our children – and if we can get on well with their children. And you can't work these things out overnight – it takes time. The whole 'getting to know you' process can take much longer than we expect because, after all, there is much more to know about them.

> **Tip for success**
> Be patient – it may take much longer for your
> new partner to build a relationship with an older child
> than with a younger one.

Carol

I first married in 1985 and have three boys aged fifteen, thirteen and eleven. My ex-husband left me for his PA who was ten years younger than me. I felt so rejected that almost immediately I threw myself into a very turbulent relationship that lasted for nearly a year. The result of all this was an extremely painful and damaging time for me and my boys. The one thing I learned is that once we have children we can't enter into relationships, let alone marriage, lightly.

I first met Tony, my second husband, when I approached him for a loan! He's a bank manager and, you guessed it, I didn't get it! But we married four years ago and between us we now have four boys and one girl aged between eleven and eighteen. We believe we've been given a second chance to enjoy a married relationship and to bring up children within a family context. But it hasn't always been and it won't always be a bed of roses – quite a lot of thorns actually.

The day we told our children we were going to get married, Tony's daughter cornered me and said, 'You won't be a wicked stepmother, will you!'

Cinderella

A recent study in *The Times* showed that mothers spend less money on food for their stepchildren than they do for their biological children. There is no inherent and natural reason for stepparents to love, or even like, their stepchildren. We have no in-built biological connection to them. We are naturally forgiving of our own children – it's just there inside us – but this does not necessarily naturally extend to stepchildren.

Whatever you may think of your stepchildren, by living with one of their parents you are bound to want to do your best for them. It's a whole package. Sometimes that may mean doing your best by an act of will. Don't assume that you will automatically love your partner's children – they will be a constant reminder of a previous relationship – as will your own children. If you can be caring and interested in your step-children's lives – however they respond to you – you'll be building long-term bridges.

Many children have a secret hope that their natural parents will be reunited, no matter how unrealistic this might be. Children want to see their parents live happily ever after. Taking this into consideration, it's obvious why a child won't immediately bond with a new stepparent. The stepparent is a barrier to her own parents getting back together. That's the bad news. The good news is you can have a successful stepfamily. It's not an easy undertaking and it should be entered into with careful consideration.

Tip for success
Always try to do your best for your stepchildren
– even if you think they don't like you!

Some advice compiled by single parents who now have new partners

1. The normal, acute, grieving period for bereavement is said to be about two years, and divorce – or splitting up – is very similar to bereavement. So think about waiting after a break-up/divorce before you enter into another long-term relationship.
2. Prepare your children tactfully and gradually. Let them know there's someone special in your life, but reassure

them that your love for them hasn't changed. Be honest –
don't try to hide your relationship. Children are much too
aware, and they always know what's going on! Answer
their questions. Introduce their future stepparent. Allow
them their feelings. Acknowledge that their feelings are
valid. Encourage them to voice their feelings even if it's,
'He's absolutely ghastly, Mum! How could you do it?'
Blending two families together will involve physical and
emotional upheaval. It may involve moving home and
moving schools. If it begins to look as though this
relationship may be a long-term one, introduce changes
gradually wherever possible. Allow stepsiblings to get to
know each other. If you can afford it, go on a family
holiday together.

3. Marry for love and shared interests, and not security.
When two parents remarry they have to cope with their
own and someone else's children who are already along
the path to adulthood. If your partner's children are older
than yours, then you're immediately into deeper water
than you are used to. All these changes are taking place
while you are trying to grow and develop another
relationship. It's a bit like doing a crash course on
marriage and parenting all at once, but with no time! In
circumstances like this we need to express our love for
each other more than ever so that we can support each
other through all the changes.

4. Be certain that your partner gets on with your children as
well as with you. They needn't love them (although it's
only natural to hope that, one day, they will) but they
must be able to be kind and civil to them. They must also
be prepared to work hard at building a relationship with
them.

5. Be prepared for your children to constantly test you and
your new partner. They will be wary of this new
relationship and will probably see it as fair game to test the

boundaries. Your children will have had you to themselves – so why should they share you with anyone else?

6. Be prepared for your partner's children to initially dislike you. Don't underestimate the emotional investment that they have in their own parents. Give them time and don't rush them.

7. Try to see things from the children's point of view. Joining a ready-made family can feel like arriving in a foreign country! They will feel overwhelmed to begin with. You will all have to find out what each other likes, what you don't like, what you find funny, the things you find interesting. It's a whole new learning curve.

8. Expect to spend a lot more time and energy on your children and stepchildren. Don't despair if there are tantrums, sulking, slamming doors, anger, jealousy, game-playing – it's part of the settling-down process and you have to go through it. But it does eat up a lot of energy – it's exhausting. You just have to try to break through, and you have to keep your own children's relationships going at the same time.

Round Two

If you intend to settle with a new partner then it's very beneficial for everyone concerned to involve your child from the outset. Don't make decisions in isolation from them, particularly if it involves a change in their living environment. There may be several children whose opinions need to be taken into account – especially if both you and your partner have children from previous relationships. It is far too big a decision for children of any age to be responsible for but it is vital that you take on board their feelings and that they *know* you have taken them on board. Listen to what your children have to say on the matter and make your decision based on a proper grasp of everyone's point of view.

Tip for success

If you think your new relationship is becoming serious,
discuss your relationship with your children at the
earliest opportunity.

Susie has remarried and her stepchildren come to stay at
weekends. This creates a set of complicated dynamics:

> *When my stepchildren come to stay for the weekend, I get in
> the smooth orange juice for one of them, chocolate ice cream
> for another and curry for the eldest. Then one of my own
> children says, 'Mum, I hate curry . . .'*
>
> *I remember the first Christmas we had together. We were
> all getting along quite happily until it came to the evening of
> Christmas Eve. We always open one present on Christmas
> Eve, but one of Simon's children said, 'I don't want to, we
> never open our presents before Christmas Day.' And one of
> my children said, 'But we always do', at which point Simon's
> daughter shot out of the room in tears. You can't think of
> everything; you just have to do the best you can. In the end
> I'm afraid we stuck with tradition. And the next year she
> was there quite happily ripping open a present on Christmas
> Eve.*

Things can only get better

In time, stepchildren can become really good friends with their
new parent. And they can become good friends with their
stepbrothers and stepsisters. Families aren't built overnight – it
takes years of shared experiences, holidays and the normal
routines of life to grow a family.

Some families bond quicker than others – through shared
interests. You may find that your partner and your children
have hobbies they can share – music, football, art – things you
may not be interested in at all! Your stepchildren will add a new

dimension to your life – and your new partner will add a new dimension to your children's lives. Through your relationship with your partner you can provide the children with a positive image of parenthood. And there are great benefits for all the children and stepchildren of an extended family – particularly as they get older. It may be hard work for you but all your children will reap the rewards.

Best laid plans

However well intentioned and however much love, time and thought we have put into a relationship, we have no guarantees that it will work out. Sadly, relationships do flounder even when both partners have put everything they have into them. If this happens you will need to stop and take stock:

- Be honest with yourself.
- What didn't work?
- And what *did* work?
- How did you contribute to the successes and failures of the relationship?

If we're honest with ourselves, we will be more likely to be able to put any mistakes behind us and move on. We need to be honest with our children as well – they may be disappointed, too, that things didn't work out. It's important that we talk to our children and find out how they're feeling. It's also important that we give our children lots of reassurance as we adjust to a new set of circumstances.

Tip for success
It takes time to adjust to change, so be kind to yourself.

Dedication, that's what you need

There are many suggestions in this life regarding what 'makes the world go round' and, for me, one of the biggest ingredients is our relationships with one another. From the security of strong emotional relationships, which are built on mutual respect and understanding, we can find stability and a sense of achievement in passing on this stability to our children. Such relationships succeed by hard work and determination rather than by chance. But by honesty, commitment, forgiveness and a large dose of sheer perseverance, we can demonstrate to our children the strength that can be derived from friendships that last.

10
The Last Word

Meant to be together...

As I gaze through my window, the trees at the bottom of the garden are beginning to let go of their leaves; the night's dew is still heavy on the ground and there is a faint smell of autumn hanging in the air. Nature, it seems, has an inevitable way of reminding us that time *never* stands still. Just as we begin to settle into a new season, yet again we are taken by surprise as the next season rises up on the horizon. So it is with parenting. The 'seasons' of our children's lives tumble seamlessly from one into another – often catching us completely unawares.

I am acutely conscious that, during the passage of writing this book, both Justine and I have become different people and that our relationship has developed and changed . . . The inevitable truth is, it will continue to do so. We are all on a journey and every step, every new experience and every decision has the potential to shape or change the direction of the next. The immense beauty of this is that it is never too late to transform the relationships we have with our children. Each new day brings new opportunities.

Few of us would argue that, whatever our family 'shape', parenting is simple and most would agree that those of us solely responsible for our children's care need extra portions of any and every virtue going!

Researching this book has opened my eyes even wider to the tough and sometimes endless uphill struggles so many of us single parents have in juggling our time, money, care and love while fulfilling every role that needs to be fulfilled. I am also convinced, more than ever before, that parenting in whatever form was never meant to be a solitary affair. 'Family', in the last century, has shrunk beyond recognition, and isolation is all too common a fact, let alone a feeling. So investing in a support network is, I believe, crucial for survival. Few of us can survive alone and I know that any degree of 'success' I can claim in my parenting is to be shared with those who have taken even a few steps of the journey with me.

In less than two years Justine will be 'officially' embarking on her own journey into adulthood, and I know that even in this short season before her eighteenth birthday I will continue to struggle with decisions and choices in my attempt to do the best for her. But I also know that few, if any, things I do in life will reap greater rewards than those I receive as the privilege of being a parent – single or otherwise.

I glance around the kitchen at the dirty dishes – courtesy mainly of Justine – stacked high on the draining board. Justine's washing lurks in piles on the floor (she has just returned from two weeks camping) and there is the unmistakable thud of Justine's music penetrating the floorboards! These occupational hazards of teenagers often try my tolerance but today at least I smile, with the realisation that I would be relieved if, on looking back, these were my biggest parenting problems!

I'm well aware that my single-parenting journey is unique – just as yours is. I also know that the ongoing journey for each and every one of us will present different challenges and joys. And yet, we all share at least one common goal and that is to continually do the best we can. As for being a success – well, I for one am grateful that the yardstick for 'successful parenting' is as ambiguous as beauty is in the eye of the beholder!

Every now and then we may have the honour of glimpsing not so much success, but a small encouraging sign that we haven't got it all completely wrong. I enjoyed one such moment a while ago and my deepest desire is that every parent has a moment such as this . . .

A few weeks back Justine and I were snuggled up on the sofa looking through a family photo album. After pausing for a while over a photo of her 'real' mum (my sister) Justine paid me *the* greatest compliment . . .

> . . . *Mum, I am very sad my real mum died and I wished that hadn't happened, and I'm sad I never really knew her and I know that things aren't always great, but in a way, Mum – you and I – I just know we are meant to be together . . .*

Further Information

Organisations

Parentalk
PO Box 23142
London SE1 OZT

Tel: 020 7450 9073
Fax: 020 7450 9060
e-mail: info@parentalk.co.uk
Website: www.parentalk.co.uk

Provides a range of resources and services designed to inspire parents to enjoy parenthood.

Care for the Family
PO Box 488
Cardiff CF15 7YY

Tel: 029 2081 0800
Fax: 029 2081 4089
e-mail: mail@cff.org.uk
Website: www.care-for-the-family.org.uk

Provides support for families through seminars, resources and special projects.

Child Benefit Centre
Department for Work and Pensions
Child Benefit Centre (Washington)
PO Box 1
Newcastle-upon-Tyne NE88 1AA

Tel: 0870 155 5540
e-mail: child-benefit@dwp.gsi.gov.uk
Website: www.dwp.gov.uk

Administers all child benefits claims.

Child Support Agency
PO Box 55
Brierley Hill
West Midlands DY5 1YL
Tel: 08457 133133 (enquiry line)

In Northern Ireland:
Great Northern Tower
17 Great Victoria Street
Belfast BT2 7AD
Tel: 08457 139896

The Government agency that assesses maintenance levels for parents who no longer live with their children.

Childalert
e-mail: info@childalert.co.uk
Website: www.childalert.co.uk

Childalert is an information service for parents and anyone else looking after children. It provides information about child safety and wellbeing in the home and on the move, covering pre-conception to the first weeks at home, to the energy and determination of toddlers, to the concerns of raising boys and girls and how different they can be.

Children 1st
83 Whitehouse Loan
Edinburgh EH9 1AT

Tel: 0131 446 2300
Fax: 0131 446 2339
e-mail: info@children1st.org.uk
Website: www.children1st.org.uk

A national Scottish voluntary organisation providing advice and support to parents on the care and protection of their children.

Citizens' Advice Bureau (CAB)
Website: www.nacab.org.uk/

A free and confidential service giving information and advice on topics such as benefits; maternity rights; debts; housing, consumer, employment and legal problems; family and personal difficulties. It also has details of useful national and local organisations. Ask at your local library or look in your phone book for your nearest office. Opening times may vary.

Contact-A-Family
209–211 City Road
London EC1V 1JN

Helpline: 0808 808 3555
Tel: 020 7608 8700
Fax: 020 7608 8701
e-mail: info@cafamily.org.uk
Website: www.cafamily.org.uk

Brings together families whose children have disabilities.

Council for Disabled Children
8 Wakley Street
London EC1V 7QE

Tel: 020 7843 6000
Fax: 020 7278 9512
e-mail: jkhan@ncb.org.uk
Website: www.ncb.org.uk

Provides an information and advice service on all matters relating to disability for children and their families.

Credit Action
6 Regent Terrace
Cambridge CB2 1AA

Helpline: 0800 591084
Tel: 01223 324034
Website: www.creditaction.com

The National Money Education Charity that promotes self-help in money education matters. Practical, sensitive and confidential advice on debt management is available via the freephone helpline. Also, a free self-help guide will be sent where appropriate. The money guide section has a good self-help guide to dealing with personal debt.

Dads & Lads
YMCA England National Dads & Lads Project
Dee Bridge House
25–27 Lower Bridge Street
Chester CH1 1RS

Tel: 01244 403090
e-mail: dirk@parenting.ymca.org.uk
ahowie@themail.co.uk

Locally based projects run jointly by YMCA and Care for the Family for fathers and sons, mentors and boys. They offer a unique opportunity to get together with other fathers and sons for a game of football and other activities. To find out where your nearest Dads & Lads project is based or to get help starting a new one, please contact Dirk Uitterdijk at the above address.

Daycare Trust

21 St George's Road
London SE1 6ES

Tel: 020 7840 3350
Website: www.daycaretrust.org.uk

Gives free advice to parents on childcare issues, promotes affordable childcare and helps you to decide what type of childcare might suit your child and family circumstances.

Fathers Direct

Herald House
Lambs Passage
Bunhill Row
London EC1Y 8TQ

Tel: 020 7920 9491
Fax: 020 7374 2966
e-mail: enquiries@fathersdirect.com
Website: www.fathersdirect.com

An information resource for fathers.

Gingerbread

7 Sovereign Close
Sovereign Court
London E1W 3HW

Advice line: 0800 018 4318 (Mon–Fri 9 a.m.–5 p.m.)
Tel: 020 7488 9300
Fax: 020 7488 9333
e-mail: office@gingerbread.org.uk
Website: www.gingerbread.org.uk

Provides day-to-day support and practical help for lone parents.

Home-Start UK
2 Salisbury Road
Leicester LE1 7QR
Tel: 0116 233 9955
Fax: 0116 233 0232
e-mail: info@home-start.org.uk
Website: www.home-start.org.uk

In Northern Ireland:
133 Bloomfield Avenue
Belfast BT5
Tel/fax: 028 9046 0772

Volunteers offer support, friendship and practical help to young families in their own homes.

Meet-A-Mum Association (MAMA)
Waterside Centre
26 Avenue Road
London SE25 4DX

Helpline: 020 8768 0123 (Mon–Fri 7–10 p.m.)
Tel: 020 8771 5595
e-mail: meet-a-mum.assoc@blueyonder.co.uk
Website: www.mama.org.uk

Provides counselling, practical support and group therapy for women suffering from post-natal depression.

National Association for Maternal and Child Welfare
40–42 Osnaburgh Street
London NW1 3ND

Tel: 020 7383 4117

Provides advice on childcare and family life.

National Autistic Society
393 City Road
London EC1V 1NG

Autism helpline: 0870 600 8585 (Mon–Fri 10 a.m.–4 p.m.)
Tel: 020 7833 2299
Fax: 020 7833 9666
e-mail: nas@nas.org.uk or autismhelpline@nas.org.uk
Website: www.nas.org.uk

Exists to champion the rights and interests of all people with autism and to ensure that they and their families receive quality services appropriate to their needs.

National Childminding Association
8 Masons Hill
Bromley
Kent BR2 9EY

Advice line: 0800 169 4486 (Mon, Tues & Thurs 10 a.m.–12 &
    2–4 p.m.; Fri 2–4 p.m.)
Tel: 020 8464 6164
Fax: 020 8290 6834
e-mail: info@ncma.org.uk
Website: www.ncma.org.uk

Informs childminders, parents and employers about the best practices in childminding.

National Council for One Parent Families
255 Kentish Town Road
London NW5 2LX

Lone Parent Line: 0800 018 5026 (Mon–Fri 9.15 a.m.–5.15 p.m.)
Maintenance & Money Line: 020 7428 5424 (Mon & Thurs
    11 a.m.–2 p.m.; Tues 3–6 p.m.)
General enquiries: 020 7428 5400
Fax: 020 7482 4851

e-mail: info@oneparentfamilies.org.uk
Website: www.oneparentfamilies.org.uk

An information service for lone parents.

National NEWPIN (New Parent and Infant Network)
Sutherland House
35 Sutherland Square
Walworth
London SE17 3EE

Tel: 020 7358 5900
Fax: 020 7701 2660
e-mail: info@newpin.org.uk
Website: www.newpin.org.uk

A network of local centres offering a range of services for parents and children.

NHS Direct
Advice line: 0845 4647
Website: www.nhsdirect.co.uk

NIPPA (The early years organisation)
6C Wildflower Way
Apollo Road
Belfast BT12 6TA

Tel: 028 9066 2825
Fax: 028 9038 1270
e-mail: mail@nippa.org
Website: www.nippa.org

Promotes high-quality early childhood care and education services.

NSPCC

Weston House
42 Curtain Road
London EC2A 3NH

Helpline: 0800 800 5000
Tel: 020 7825 2500
Fax: 020 7825 2525
Website: www.nspcc.org.uk

Aims to prevent child abuse and neglect in all its forms and give practical help to families with children at risk. The NSPCC also produces leaflets with information and advice on positive parenting – for these, call 020 7825 2500.

One Parent Families Scotland

13 Gayfield Square
Edinburgh EH1 3NX

Tel: 0131 556 3899
Fax: 0131 557 7899
e-mail: info@opfs.org.uk
Website: www.opfs.org.uk

Provides information, training, counselling and support to one-parent families throughout Scotland.

Oneplusone

The Wells
7/15 Rosebery Avenue
London EC1R 4SP

Tel: 020 7841 3660
Fax: 020 7841 3670
e-mail: info@oneplusone.org.uk
Website: www.oneplusone.org.uk

Aims to build through research a framework for understanding contemporary marriage and partnership.

Parentline Plus

520 Highgate Studios
53–76 Highgate Road
Kentish Town
London NW5 1TL

Helpline: 0808 800 2222
Textphone: 0800 783 6783
Fax: 020 7284 5501
e-mail: centraloffice@parentlineplus.org.uk
Website: www.parentlineplus.org.uk

Provides a freephone helpline called Parentline and courses for parents via the Parent Network Service. Parentline Plus also includes the National Stepfamily Association. For all information, call the Parentline freephone number: 0808 800 2222.

Parents Advice Centre

Floor 4, Franklin House
12 Brunswick Street
Belfast BT2 7GE

Helpline: 028 9023 8800
Tel: 028 9031 0891
Fax: 028 9031 2475
e-mail: belfast@pachelp.org
Website: www.pachelp.org

A voluntary organisation that offers support, guidance and counselling to parents and young people with family difficulties.

Parents Anonymous
6–9 Manor Gardens
London N7 6LA

Tel: 020 7263 8918 (Mon–Fri)

24-hour answering service for parents who feel they can't cope or feel they might abuse their children.

Parents at Work
45 Beech Street
London EC2Y 8AD

Tel: 020 7628 3565
Fax: 020 7628 3591
e-mail: info@parentsatwork.org.uk
Website: www.parentsatwork.org.uk

Provides advice and information about childcare provision.

Positive Parenting
1st Floor
2A South Street
Gosport PO12 1ES

Tel: 023 9252 8787
Fax: 023 9250 1111
e-mail: info@parenting.org.uk
Website: www.parenting.org.uk

Aims to prepare people for the role of parenting by helping parents, those about to become parents and also those who lead parenting groups.

raisingkids.co.uk
Website: www.raisingkids.co.uk

This website provides individual advice from Dr Pat Spungin and other qualified experts, a huge reference library of parenting

*solutions, plus online discussions for support from the raisingkids.
co.uk online community of parents in similar situations.*

Relate
Herbert Gray College
Little Church Street
Rugby CV21 3AP
Tel: 01788 573 241
e-mail: enquiries@national.relate.org.uk
Website: www.relate.org.uk

In Northern Ireland:
76 Dublin Road
Belfast BT2 7HP
Tel: 028 9032 3454

*Provides a confidential counselling service for relationship
problems of any kind. Local branches are listed in the phone book.*

Twins and Multiple Birth Association (TAMBA)
2 The Willows
Gardner Road
Guildford
Surrey GU1 4PG

Helpline 01732 868000 (Mon–Fri 7–11 p.m.; weekends 10 a.m.–
   11 p.m.)
Tel: 0870 770 3305
Fax: 0870 770 3303
e-mail: enquiries@tamba.org.uk
Website: www.tamba.org.uk

*Gives information and support to families with twins, triplets
and more.*

Parenting Courses

Parentalk Parenting Course

A new parenting course designed to give parents the opportunity to share their experiences, learn from each other and discover some principles of parenting. For more information, phone 020 7450 9073.

Positive Parenting

Publishes a range of low-cost, easy-to-read, common-sense resource materials that provide help, information and advice. Responsible for running a range of parenting courses across the UK. For more information, phone 023 9252 8787.

Parent Network

For more information, call Parentline Plus on 0808 800 2222.

More About Paren**T**alk

Launched in 1999, in response to research which revealed that 1 in 3 parents feel like failures, Parentalk is all about inspiring parents to make the most of their vitally important role.

A registered charity, we exist to provide relevant information and advice for mums and dads in a format that they feel most comfortable with, regardless of their background or family circumstances.

Our current activities include:

- **The Parentalk Parenting Principles Course**

  Already used by almost 25,000 mums and dads, this video-based resource brings together groups of parents to share their experiences, laugh together and learn from one another. Filmed at the studios of GMTV, endorsed by the National Confederation of Parent Teacher Associations and featuring Parentalk Founder Steve Chalke, the course is suitable for use by groups of parents in their own homes or by schools, PTAs, pre-schools and nurseries, health visitors, health centres, family centres, employers, churches and other community groups.

- **Parentalk Local Events**

  Looking at every age group from the toddler to the teenage years, and from how to succeed as a parent to how to succeed as a grandparent, Parentalk evenings are a specially tailored, fun mixture of information, shared stories and advice for success as a mum, dad or grandparent. Operating across the country, the Parentalk team of speakers can also provide input on a range of more specialist subjects such as helping your child sleep or striking a healthy balance between work and family life.

- **Parentalk at Work Events**
Parentalk offer lunchtime and half-day workshops for employers and employees, at their place of work, that look at getting the balance right between the responsibilities of work and those of a family. Parentalk also provides a life coaching service for employees, helping them to deal with the pressures they encounter at home in order to be happier, and perform better, at work.

  All Parentalk at Work initiatives are backed up by a comprehensive website: **www.parentalk.co.uk/atwork**

- **The Parentalk Guide Series**
In addition to the 'How to Succeed' series, Parentalk offers a comprehensive series of titles that look at a wide variety of parenting issues. All of these books are easy-to-read, down-to-earth and full of practical information and advice.

- **The Parentalk Schools Pack**
This resource, designed especially for year 9 pupils, builds on the success of the Parentalk Video Course, to provide material for eight lessons on subjects surrounding preparing for parenthood. The pack has been tailored to dovetail with the PHSE and citizenship curriculum and is available for teachers to download from the Parentalk website.

- **www.parentalk.co.uk**
www.parentalk.co.uk is a lively, upbeat site exclusively for parents, packed with fun ideas, practical advice and some great tips for making the most of being a mum or dad.

To find out more about any of these Parentalk initiatives or our plans for the future, or to receive our

quarterly newsletter, contact a member of the team at the address below:

Parentalk
115 Southwark Bridge Road
London SE1 0AX
Tel: 020 7450 9073
Fax: 020 7450 9060
e-mail: info@parentalk.co.uk

**Helping parents make the most of every stage
of their child's growing up.**

(Registered Charity No: 1074790)